Physical Characteristics of the Airedale Terrier
(from The Kennel Club breed standard)

Tail: Set on high and carried gaily, not curled over back. Good strength and substance. Customar'' docked. Tip approximately at the same heigh top of skull.

Hindquarters: Thighs long and powerful with muscular second thigh, stifles well bent, turned neither in nor out. Hocks well let down, parallel with each other when viewed from behind.

Body: Back short, strong, straight and level, showing no slackness. Loins muscular. Ribs well sprung. Chest deep (i. e. approximately level with elbows) but not broad.

Size: Height about 58–61 cms (23–24 ins) for dogs, taken from top of shoulder, and bitches about 56–59 cms (22–23 ins).

Feet: Small, round and compact, with a good depth of pad, well cushioned, and toes moderately arched, turning neither in nor out.

Airedale Terrier

by Bardi Mc Lennan

Table of Contents

9

Origin of the Airedale Terrier

Meet the largest of the British terriers that hails from the valley of the River Aire, whence comes his name. Learn about the Airedale's natural versatility, seen through the prism of time, as a working terrier, police and military dog and home companion and guard.

24

Characteristics of the Airedale Terrier

Discover whether or not you are an Airedale person and worthy of owning the 'King of Terriers.' See how the Airedale is not only a competent protector of property but also an accomplished hunter, a vigorous playmate and an 'oversized lapdog'!

32

Breed Standard for the Airedale Terrier

Learn the requirements of a well-bred Airedale Terrier by studying the description of the breed set forth in The Kennel Club standard. Both show dogs and pets must possess key characteristics as outlined in the breed standard.

40

Your Puppy Airedale Terrier

Be advised about choosing a reputable breeder and selecting a healthy, typical puppy. Understand the responsibilities of ownership, including home preparation, acclimatisation, the vet and prevention of common puppy problems.

70

Everyday Care of Your Airedale Terrier

Enter into a sensible discussion of dietary and feeding considerations, exercise, grooming, travelling and identification of your dog. This chapter discusses Airedale Terrier care for all stages of development.

PUBLISHED IN THE
UNITED KINGDOM BY:

INTERPET
PUBLISHING

Vincent Lane, Dorking
Surrey RH4 3YX
England

ISBN 1-902389-47-6

90

Housebreaking and Training Your Airedale Terrier

by Charlotte Schwartz
Be informed about the importance of training your Airedale Terrier from the basics of housebreaking and understanding the development of a young dog to executing obedience commands (sit, stay, down, etc.).

PHOTOS BY ISABELLE FRANCAIS
AND CAROL ANN JOHNSON
WITH ADDITIONAL PHOTOS BY:

Norvia Behling
TJ Calhoun
Carolina Biological Supply
Doskocil
Isabelle Francais
James Hayden-Yoav
James R Hayden, RBP
Bill Jonas
Alice van Kempen

Dwight R Kuhn
Dr Dennis Kunkel
Ohio Historical Society
Mikki Pet Products
Phototake
Jean Claude Revy
Dr Andrew Spielman
C James Webb

Illustrations by Renée Low

148

Showing Your Airedale Terrier

Experience the dog show world, including different types of shows and the making up of a champion. Go beyond the conformation ring to working trials and agility trials, etc.

117

Health Care of Your Airedale Terrier

Discover how to select a proper veterinary surgeon and care for your dog at all stages of life. Topics include vaccination scheduling, skin problems, dealing with external and internal parasites and the medical and behavioural conditions common to the breed.

The publisher would like to thank the following owners for allowing their dogs to be photographed for this book:

Judy Averis
Grace McKearnin
the Ricciardi family
Robert Shannon

The courageous and athletic Airedale Terrier has its origins in the valley of the Aire and Wharfe Rivers. This handsome black and tan Adonis is the largest of the British terriers.

It is certain that the Airedale Terrier originated in the valley of the Aire and Wharfe Rivers, but the breed's exact genetic makeup is conjecture at best. The creators were either blissfully unaware of the conundrum they were leaving future enthusiasts of their newly created breed or, as competitive sportsmen, took sly amusement in leaving us with a puzzle on which to place our bets.

Small terriers were used from time immemorial for poaching the fields and streams of the landed gentry. Rabbits and birds that strayed by chance beyond the gamekeeper's sharp eye were 'fair game' to the poacher in search of food for his table. Terriers had to be quick and accurate to catch this prey. They were considered 'easy keepers,' who slept by the fire or in the barn, required little in the way of food, were a healthy lot and, best of all, were extremely willing and capable workers. They also kept the rat population under control.

When the towns of Leeds, Bradford, Otley and Bingley and the surrounding area first became

Used to create the Airedale, the Otterhound is also associated with the River Aire, and is famous for its ability to hunt otters in the rough waters of the river.

industrialized in the early 1800s, the millworkers and miners were using their small terriers on the abundance of small game (primarily water rats) found along the banks of the Aire, Wharfe, Colne and Calder rivers. In a short time, the Aire itself became so heavily lined with factories and mills that the otter and fish population retreated to adjoining less-polluted waterways. The water rats remained behind.

Pursuit of the strong-swimming otters by the small terriers had never been too successful due to the terriers' short legs, which hampered their ability to wade into deep water or to swim long distances upstream. Packs of Otterhounds were the recognised leaders in this endeavour, and as such had the full support of the fishermen whose sport and food supply were being depleted by the fish-hungry otters in the rivers and streams feeding the industry-choked Aire.

The factory and mill workers considered water-ratting a prime weekend sport. Organised matches generated such keen competition that spectators lined the river banks to wager on their favourites. The dogs were sent out two at a time and points were scored for speed and performance in both locating and in dispatching the rats.

A CLEVER SOLUTION

It wasn't long before some bright lads hit upon the idea of mating the gameness of the terrier with the aquatic ability of the hound as the answer to extending their sport. No doubt they also reasoned that one or two such offspring could be kept at home as were their small terriers, rather than requiring the large kennelling facilities needed for packs of Otterhounds. Wilfred Holmes is credited with having made the first such cross of hound

DID YOU KNOW?

A 'working terrier' used to refer only to a terrier that worked underground. Today, however, small underground terriers are commonly called 'earth dogs' and all terriers, large and small, that do work of any kind be it Search and Rescue, sniffing narcotics, chasing lions or rabbits, are referred to as 'working terriers.' To be sure, there are still hold-outs for the original definition!

and terrier in 1853.

At this point I would like to hypothesize. We know the Black and Tan Terrier (whether you wish to call it English or Welsh) was the common terrier in the area. Therefore, would not the Welsh Harrier have been an obvious choice for a cross to obtain slightly more leg and the strength to work in water? In his book *Hounds of The World*, Sir John Buchanan-Jardine, Bt, MFH, MBH, describes the Welsh Hound, or Harrier, of the 1800s as black and tan or red with rough or wire hair, and smaller than its English cousins. He adds this, which would indicate a perfect trait to cross with a terrier: '(Welsh Harriers) hunt in a more indepen-dent style, taking nothing for

granted and relying mostly on their own individual efforts.' This was (and is) contrary to the pack hunting style of the English hounds and of the Otterhounds. Then there is the suspicion put forth by Otterhound authorities that the Welsh Harrier is in their ancestral heap!

So we have the wire-coated Welsh Terrier whose coloration was always black and tan or red

and so affirmed in writings of the 1400s. We have the harsh-coated Welsh Harrier, always black and tan or red, but smaller than the Otterhound, which at that time rose to 68.5 cms (27 ins) and

> **DID YOU KNOW?**
> The Kennel Club Stud Book was published in 1874 to register dogs by breed, but the problems with breed classifications persisted. In 1890, for example, at Crufts, there was one class listed that wasn't for any breed at all! Class #220 was for 'Stuffed dogs, or dogs made of wood, china, etc.' This may have been the forerunner of the dog show concessionaire.

This drawing from 1849 shows Harriers, which some believe played a part in the development of the Airedale Terrier.

The extinct Black and Tan Terriers, shown in this 1881 drawing, were common to the area from which the Airedale emanated and are believed to have contributed to the development of many modern terriers.

Weston Pilot was a Harrier that became a winner of the Championship Cup in 1928. Unfortunately, the markings are not clear in this old photo, but the dog had the distinctive black saddle.

Airedale Terrier

weighed as much as 54.46 kgs (120 lbs)! The weight of the Waterside or Bingley Terrier, as the Airedale was first known, averaged 15.9–20.44 kgs (35–45 lbs). Today's Airedale weighs about 27.2 kgs (60 lbs).

Now then, were the first Hound crosses the Welsh or the Otter? We shall never know!

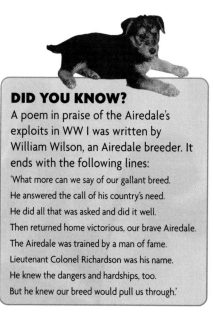

DID YOU KNOW?

A poem in praise of the Airedale's exploits in WW I was written by William Wilson, an Airedale breeder. It ends with the following lines:

'What more can we say of our gallant breed.
He answered the call of his country's need.
He did all that was asked and did it well.
Then returned home victorious, our brave Airedale.
The Airedale was trained by a man of fame.
Lieutenant Colonel Richardson was his name.
He knew the dangers and hardships, too.
But he knew our breed would pull us through.'

TO CONTINUE...

These first Airedale breeders were intent on the results being nothing more or less than a terrier. What of the 'other terriers' frequently mentioned as outcrosses used to eliminate what were considered to be undesirable hound characteristics, such as heavy low-set ears, rounded skull, light eyes, slow hound-like gait and soft woolly coat? (These atavistic faults, by the way, appear from time to time in Airedales to this day.) It is difficult to imagine just how the Bull Terrier (one of those cited) would have corrected these matters, but it might have contributed substance. The Black and Tan Terrier had originally been selected for its drive, tenacity and punishing jaws, so they did not need the Bull Terrier for those attributes. Despite the geographic proximity and the fact that these breeds were not then what we see today, introducing the Dandie Dinmont Terrier would seem an unlikely choice to produce the desired coat, colour or ear type. Some records of the day lay claim to such mixes, while others refute it.

As late as 1930, a noted writer

The famous painting 'The Airedale,' rendered by the skilled dog artist Mrs Scott-Langley in 1933, is typical of the good quality Airedales of the period.

dismissed the breed as rather useless, saying, 'Their coats are not heavy enough for them to act as retrievers in cold weather and their noses are not good enough for them to follow cold trails.'

Other observers at the time held an opposing view. One commented on the Airedale's exceptional capability 'not only to hunt vermin but also to hunt game and to retrieve it as well, as he has a very keen nose and is a remarkably good water dog.' As time went on, this latter view prevailed and holds today.

ENTER THE SHOW DOG

The first dog shows moved from pubs and parlours to become part of the popular agricultural shows. In the mid-1860s, this new breed caught on at shows in nearby Otley, Shipley, Keighly and

DID YOU KNOW?

In World War I, Germany already had some 50,000 dogs trained for military duty when the war broke out. England hastily recruited and trained 2,000 dogs, including Airedale Terriers, for work at the front with the troops. Dogs that failed the intense training were honourably discharged (sent home). American forces did not have dogs in the military then, but they did by WWII. To prove the worth of these war dogs, Hitler had an estimated 30,000 German Shepherd Dogs ready for action by the outbreak of WWII and Russia topped all nations with a canine military force estimated at over a million!

'Pioneer of the Airedale Terrier,' as this old woodcut was titled, depicts Young Tanner from the 1880s, typical of how the early Airedale Terriers appeared.

Bingley first as Waterside Terriers, then as Bingley Terriers. Indeed, the first presentations in Otley and Bingley brought a crowd of admiring spectators to ringside and the public's acclaim of the breed has not wavered since.

In 1882, Hugh Dalziel, a well-known judge and dog writer, chaired a meeting of the Dales terriermen at the Airedale Agricultural Society Show held at Bingley. It was finally decided to settle the name debate and the suggestion of Airedale Terrier was agreed upon to represent the entire area rather than a single town.

The breed was entered as the Airedale Terrier in the National Dog Show at Birmingham in 1883 and three years later was officially accepted in The Kennel Club Stud Book. One still had to remain alert in tracing a dog's lineage because the names of the dogs changed as

At the turn of the 20th century, Airedales were trained in police work. Here the famed Lt Col. E H Richardson is teaching an Airedale Terrier to climb a ladder to attack an assassin.

Matador Mandarin was a British champion from the 1930s who, supposedly, was purchased for a few shillings as a pet and later went on to win many show awards.

often as did the owners. In those days, there were no restrictions regarding a dog's name or the owner's kennel affix.

There is inevitably one person in any given breed who stands out as what today would be called the breed's first publicist, one whose writing ability and contagious enthusiasm for the breed make the world sit up and take notice. In the history of the Airedale Terrier, Holland Buckley of Burnham, Bucks was that person.

Mr Buckley wrote *The Airedale Terrier*, the first book dedicated solely to the breed and its early history. He writes of the confusion that existed in many breeds due to the lack of breeding records.

In the latter half of the 1800s when dog shows were still in their infancy, breed classifications were not necessarily specific. The Broken-haired Terrier class, for example, took in just about anything that would visually fit that description. Pedigrees were often non-existent or imprecise: 'Ben, sired by Green's Jim out of

Nan' would leave anyone save a close friend of Mr Green's completely in the dark as to the lineage. Mr Buckley tells of one dog having been awarded prizes as an Old English Black and Tan Terrier and as a Welsh Terrier although both parents were known to be Airedales, something not at all uncommon at the time.

By now the breed was definitely all terrier, but at 15.9–20.44 kgs (35–45 lbs), it was well beyond the size to 'go to earth,' or *terra firma,* for which all 'terriers' are named. The larger size, however, proved to have definite benefits. Longer legs meant the dogs could work in water along the riverbanks without having to swim, while their strong deep chest enabled them to swim a fair distance when necessary. In the fields, longer legs allowed the dogs to clamber over stiles and other obstacles without having to be picked up

15

Airedale Terrier

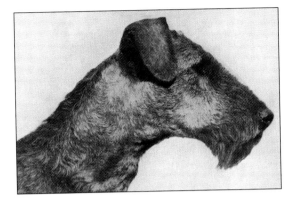

and carried.

Still, both the size and the terrier designation were disputed. Some felt the dogs should be considered hounds or (horrors!) crossbreeds. Initially, as one would expect, in any given litter some pups might display hound features, and others those of the terrier, lending credence to the crossbreed stand. Of course the Airedale was a mix, but almost every breed of dog in the world which was developed by man for a specific purpose began life as a crossbreed.

A STANDARD, OF SORTS

The first breed standard with a scale of points was written in 1879 by Reginald Knight of Leeds and based entirely on his dog, Thunder, whom he considered to be almost perfect. Great controversy ensued and a second standard and points scale were drawn up by a group of breeders who felt, despite Mr Knight's

understandable devotion to Thunder, there was still much work required to bring the breed to anything like their idea of perfection.

A dog named Colne Crack was among the first thought to be without most of the undesirable hound-like features. A bitch by Crack and out of Poll was named Fracture. (You begin to see how 'specific' this background information is.) Fracture is described as having a soft coat and bad ears, but nevertheless did some early winning. The leading stud dog of the day was Rover III, whelped in 1881. He sired several champions, including Venus III and Vixen III. Another, Cholmondeley Bondsman, is best known for having been sold for 100 guineas, an outrageous sum in that era. Things were looking up for the new breed.

However, a dog named simply Airedale Jerry is felt to be the first of the breed as we would recognise it today. We do know how Jerry came about. A dog named Bruce sired Ch Brush (before Bruce was sent off to America in 1881) and Brush's daughter, Bess was bred to Rattler to produce Jerry in 1888.

Jerry was bred to Cholmondeley Luce, a mating that produced another great one, Cholmondeley Briar, a top dog in his lifetime. Briar was the only pup in his litter to survive. Another example of the name-change-syndrome: Briar was entered as Red Robin at the Bingley show where he took first prize at the age of six months and at which time he was sold and the name changed. Briar went on to win 100 consecutive firsts and was considered by many to be the 'father of the breed,' a designation given to several of the first top sires. Among the bitches that did well was Luce (also called Miss Luce), whose next litter became all first-prize winners and all but one in her third litter repeated this feat.

Briar, mated to a Ch Newbold Test daughter, Rosamond, sired Briar Test, a dog considered for type to be an even more dominant 'father of the breed.' Test's son, Master Briar, bred to a daughter of Holland Buckley's Clonmel Marvel produced Ch Clonmel

PHOTO COURTESY OF THE OHIO HISTORICAL SOCIETY.

DID YOU KNOW?
US President Warren Harding's Airedale, Laddie Boy, had his own hand-carved Cabinet chair where he sat during important conferences, and was also allowed the distinction of greeting dignitaries on the front steps of the White House. The press had great fun pretending to interview the dog on political questions. When

President Harding died in 1923, thousands of newsboys donated pennies that were melted down and cast into a statue of Laddie Boy, which stands today in the Smithsonian Institute in Washington, DC.

Airedale Terrier

This is believed to be the first published illustration of an Airedale: Thunder, owned by R Knight, drawn in 1878.

Monarch. Ch Warland What Not and Int Ch Warland Ditto were two from J P Hall's kennels that were held to be exceptional. Ditto's get figured prominently in England, on the Continent and in America.

AMERICA, A PRIME MARKET

Through these close lines came all the top Airedales of the early 1900s, including virtually every good representative of the breed that was to be the foundation of the leading Airedale kennels in America. And still comments persisted about size, light eyes, soft coat—and those ears!

Although the dog Bruce arrived in the US in 1881 (three years prior to the founding of the American Kennel Club), it wasn't until Ch Clonmel Marvel won the breed at Westminster in 1900 and repeated the win the following year that the Airedale Terrier was accepted as a rising star on American soil. These wins were followed by another two of Mr Buckley's dogs—Ch Clonmel Bed Rock and Ch Clonmel Monarch, this latter being the dog Buckley

himself deemed to be closest to perfection. Even though the dog had sired many litters before going to America, Buckley was harshly criticised for letting this prized dog leave England.

It is interesting to note the pride with which imports were touted in the US and Canada. Owning or breeding show dogs began to carry the prestige of owning race horses. One man advertised that he was the first to introduce and exhibit these dogs in the US (an unconfirmed statement), while another offered 'the most successful Airedales living.' Another breeder, the proud owner of Briar Ranger (from Cholmondeley Briar), noted the dog to be 'full of the most valuable blood' and for more emphasis added, 'all stock recently imported from England.'

MOVING ON

At the onset of World War I, the Airedale Terrier became England's war dog, in part to overcome the stigma of enemy attached to the German Shepherd Dog (Alsatian). Shows were halted, pursuits of championships put on hold, but the breed's military accomplishments in battle won it a permanent place in the hearts of the public. Word of mighty feats performed by Airedales at the front spread to America and as a result some of the best dogs in Britain were sold to the US for large sums of money. Among them were several of J P Hall's 'Warland' dogs, including Int Ch Warland Ditto, a top sire appearing in pedigrees of most leading kennels of the day.

Top breeders in the British Isles have always sold their 'good ones.' The reason given is that the British breeders are generally in it for life, often passing the kennels along to their offspring, whereas in other countries, particularly in America, show folk last about six years. They are apt to give up if in five years they haven't handled, bred or bought a Best in Show dog, or perhaps the care of dogs 365 days a year takes its toll. Breeders in Britain are not so competitive, but as perpetual optimists, they believe that the 'perfect' pup is sure to be in the next litter.

One of the undesirable features agreed upon by all in the early years (along with light eyes and long ears) was the persistence of faded colour and soft texture of the coat. After WWI, a dog named Ch Mespot Tinker, found as a pup by A J Edwards, was a force in establishing what was wanted. He was highly acclaimed for his jet-black saddle and rich red tan jacket of the correct wire texture. Even more significant, he was prepotent for both, passing these traits along to his offspring. It seems the striking deep colour was what most attracted people to

the breed.

A J 'Towyn' Edwards was well known as an exceptionally fine breeder of both Welsh and Fox Terriers. And where do you suppose Mr Edwards found Mespot Tinker? In Aberdovey, Wales—right where those small black and red Welsh Terriers had been for centuries! And from where (I'm delighted to add), according to historian J L Ethel Aspinall, came the contribution of the Welsh Harrier to the Airedale Terrier mix (Miss Aspinall grew up in Scotland and her affix, Llanipsa, was not Welsh, but merely her surname spelled backwards!).

Women were taking their place in the dog world. Mrs M Beamish-Levy, in addition to running her Ardross kennels, founded a training college for kennelmaids. George Oliver and

During World War I, British troops used Airedales to carry messenger pigeons to a given point and then release them in order to communicate with troops under siege.

his wife were both Airedale enthusiasts, with Mrs Oliver founding the North of England ATC in 1923. This trend continues, with huge numbers of women in the UK, on the Continent and elsewhere in the world not only breeding Airedales but grooming them and handling them in the show ring.

A PERILOUS SETBACK

By the early 1920s, the breed had become too popular for its own good. Would-be breeders, who knew nothing about dogs, the breeding of them, or the Airedale Terrier's temperament or needs, took to producing them en masse. Their only goal was to profit from selling puppies. Their lack of integrity created a glut on the market and in shelters. Poorly bred and poorly raised, many of these dogs were aggressive, with untypical coats and ears (of course) and with a variety of health problems. This situation was particularly bad in America. To this day, many uninformed people still consider the Airedale to be an aggressive guardian of its turf. So be it. No doubt that misconception has deterred many an intruder!

By the end of the 1920s, the demand had dried up and the profiteers retreated. A number of concerned breeders assumed the task of eliminating the problems caused by uninformed over-breeding, as well as putting right the Airedale's deteriorating public image. The comeback was slow but steady, and extremely gratifying. By the end of the 1930s, the Airedale Terrier once again stood as the undoubted King of Terriers—a sensible protector, willing worker, playful prankster and faithful friend.

Today there are many good English kennels, and three outstanding ones. Olive Jackson's Jokyl affix is recognised worldwide. Ch Jokyl Hot and Spicey is one of her top dogs. Judith Averis and David Scawthorne's Ch Saredon Lightning Strikes is also a representative of an outstanding English kennel, along with dogs from the Stargus kennels of Mrs Lesley Lee.

THE AIREDALE AT HOME AND ABROAD

There were no Championship Shows during the two World Wars, 1915 to 1919 and again 1938 to 1945. Breeding also slowed down, but the clubs remained active and overseas sales of dogs from the UK picked up quickly, especially after 1945.

Mollie Harmsworth's Bengal affix lives on in numerous pedigrees throughout the world. Ch Bengal Sabu was not shown in England, but his outstanding success as a show dog and sire in America in the 1960s brought him to the attention of breeders. However, it was his silly side that endeared him to all who knew him. One such moment is captured in Barbara Strebeigh's amusing snapshots of the great Sabu sporting a full American Indian feather headdress while riding a child's tricycle. His temperament did much to popularise the breed.

George and Olive Jackson (Jokyl) bred or owned 50 champions from 1958 to 1992, and a Jokyl dog or bitch was sire or dam of an additional 30! And the list goes on. Given that only eight to ten champions are made up in the breed each year, this is truly a great record. One dog, bred by Mrs Harmsworth and owned by the Jacksons, Jokyl Bengal Figaro, was a film star in America, then (based in Germany) toured the Continent and became the first truly international champion Airedale before returning to the UK. Ch Jokyl Gallipants was a particular standout in Airedale history, earning Top Dog all breeds in 1983, Top Airedale in 1984, Top Airedale Sire in 1985 and Top Terrier Sire in 1986!

The Airedale is presently popular throughout the world, with all his related activities strongly supported by active club members. In Italy, Airedales are classified as Guard Dogs, not Terriers, perhaps only by definition limiting their other capabili-

ties. Since 1945 Airedales have twice taken the Supreme Champion title at Crufts Dog Show. The millennium celebration of the Airedale Terrier, from 23–25 June, 2000 in Bingley, would surely mark one of the great milestones of the breed.

Strict rules in Germany govern all breeding of purebred dogs. The three- to five-day-old litter is inspected by a breed 'specialist' from the National Kennel Club who checks each puppy and the breeder is allowed to keep only the best; the others are destroyed. Despite this, Germany boasts the Airedale as one of their most popular Terrier breeds with members of Klub für Terrier active in all aspects of breeding, showing and guard-dog training. Dogs in Germany and in Finland must prove their working

Prized for their vigilant guarding ability, Airedales have been used to protect exclusive stores for decades. This Airedale is guarding a famous jewelry boutique in London.

ability before making up champions. Dr Hannibal-Friedrich's multiple title holder, Headhunter von der Locher Muhle, not only is siring winning puppies on the Continent but also has promising litters in the US via frozen semen.

In 1894 the first (English) Airedale appeared in a Swedish dog show in Stockholm. The breed was slow to catch on, but with imports from England and Germany, the Airedale population rose steadily. Stig Ahlberg (Ragtime), the 'father of Swedish Airedales,' owned the bitch Ch Drakehall Dinah, who was Best in Show at the Centenary Show in 1976. Ahlberg is a highly sought-after judge in the US and Europe. Among today's breeders, Pia and Stefan Lundberg (Pinto) are as successful at home as are their exports to Australia. Tail docking is currently banned in Sweden, but as in other countries where the ban has been in effect, there is a strong movement gaining ground to once again allow tail docking.

A vital venture in Norway is the snow rescue service by the Red Cross and police in which Airedales have proven their diverse capabilities. An Airedale fortuitously named Doctor Lavin was whelped in 1979. After years of training, he passed his Avalanche Rescue Tests in 1984 and was made up a champion the next year. He also competed in agility and continued with rescues, living this full life until the age of 13.

One Airedale in Denmark stands out, not only as Top Dog in 1995 and 1996, but for the number of titles he has won for his owner, Mrs Rita Ahle Erichsen. He is Int Ch Am Ch, DKCh, SuCh, VDCh, KfTCh, KLBCh Darbywood's Preferred Stock. Bred by Jean Surfus, 'Stockton' is by Ch Epoch's Nineteen Eighty-Four ex Ch Darbywood's Eye of the Tiger. Stockton also won the Best Terrier Progeny Class at the European Dog Show in Copenhagen in 1997. The Scandinavian countries are looking forward to the relaxation of quarantine laws to permit easier breeding of desirable dogs and to participate in top competition.

In Finland the breed is known as keen hunters of every type of prey from mice to elk. They are also active in agility, obedience and working trials (and must pass working tests before being granted a championship), proving them truly successful all-purpose dogs. Finland even boasts a summer camp for Airedale Terriers and their owners. Currently, Pirjo Hjelm's Big Lady kennels has some of the best dogs in the country.

Stringent rules also govern

the breeding of dogs in Russia. Permission must be obtained from a Club Council for every mating, or the resulting litter cannot be shown. Russia began with bloodlines from many famous English kennels, but in the 1990s leaned heavily on US imports such as the Russian Best in Show winner Ch Spindletop's Desperado, a littermate to the US's top Airedale, Ch Spindletop's New Kid In Town, bred by Anne Reese. Desperado is owned by Valentine Egorova of Saratov. Other top American dogs have gone to Helen Kukoleva (Emerald Dalikul) from Aletta Moore (Epoch).

There is a little controversy at present with the 'old school' preferring the old-style bigger, slightly longer bodied dogs with extremely hard coats and gorgeous heads, mostly coming down from Bengal and Mynair stock. The newer generation of breeders goes for dogs termed 'Western-style' or those bred from American imports. The latter have managed to retain the good heads, which may mean Russian imports will be appearing on the American show scene.

Airedales in Australian shows were originally shown in 'the rough.' The first trimmed dogs were shown by L Latchford (Aerial) in 1918 and created quite a stir, although everyone quickly followed suit. More recently, several kennels have been outstandingly successful, among them Mrs Pauline Lewis' Moylarg, Mrs Geisla Lesh's Strongfort, Bob and Jane Harvey's Rangeaire, Keith and Patricia Lovell's Tjuringa and David and Di Barclay's York Park.

Ch Brentleigh Ben Nevis, CD became a breed legend. He was the top winner for three consecutive years and was the first Airedale in Victoria to earn an obedience title. Although Ben Nevis died very young (age seven), he left behind 18 champions; 2 sons went on to earn CDX degrees and another led the life of a fox hunter and never saw the show ring but sired several champions.

Japan has been smitten by the Airedale since the 1920s. The Japan Airedale Terrier Society was founded in 1930 with most of their stock coming from England. Barely 30 dogs survived WW II, but a sufficient number of good dogs have been imported since to assure their future. In Japan, Airedales serve on the police force.

America has had a long love affair with the Airedale. Many pet owners go from childhood to retirement with one Airedale after another. The Airedale Terrier Club of America was founded in 1900, the enthusiastic result of early importers of this 'new' terrier breed.

The Airedale Terrier is a good-sized dog with a large personality. Two traits common to the breed go hand in hand: self-confidence and the desire to dominate. He's also fearless to a fault, stoic, loyal, tenacious, intensely curious, intelligent and with a lively sense of mischief. These traits spell out a dog that is not for the faint of heart nor for the weak of resolve. The Airedale must be persuaded, not coerced, into following the rules firmly, consistently and nicely. Anyone with similar characteristics or who admires and can cope with such strong traits will make a good owner.

He is not a go-to-ground terrier for obvious reasons. He is too big to enter the den of a hedgehog or polecat, but he can and will dispatch any prey immediately if it bolts. As any owner is quick to cite, the Airedale's true terrier fondness for the earth is deep. Sometimes it goes very deep—excavating huge holes in the garden in pursuit of real or imaginary prey!

Unlike many of his smaller terrier cousins, he is not hyperactive and matures at about three years of age into a calm house dog. Affable and amusing as a companion, he's also sensitive to raised voices or harsh corrections.

Some of these terrier attributes will stand in the way of anyone who mistakenly thinks an Airedale will be a pushover as a pet. His tenacious spirit may be mistaken for stubbornness and thus mishandled. His intelligence allows the dog to outwit you, and it is not so easy to maintain discipline over a dog whose feelings you've hurt. Just when you're about to clamp down for some misbehaviour, he turns on the charm. Oh well, maybe you'll catch him to make the correction next time. It can be difficult to keep one step ahead of an Airedale.

ARE YOU AN AIREDALE PERSON?

If you've never met an adult Airedale, the time to do so is before you've decided on this breed. For good measure, meet more than one. Attend dog shows and chat with breeders. Visit breeders where you can spend time in the house or garden with adult dogs. It's not enough to view them through a kennel fence.

Not every good dog owner is necessarily the right person to own an Airedale Terrier. For starters, he's a medium-to-large dog, about 58 cms (23 ins) at shoulder and ranging anywhere from 20.4 kgs to 29.5 kgs (45 to 65 lbs). Therefore the owner must be physically able to handle a dog of this size and strength. Then add the ability to cope with—and thoroughly enjoy—the Airedale's playful, exuberant personality. Finally, there is the need to accept a dog as a lifetime commitment. If you start off with a puppy, it will remain a puppy for 18 months, it will be a young adult for another 18 months and will continue to share your life for about another 10 years.

The Airedale is a protector of property, but will not necessarily stay on its own property. Solo expeditions by these hunters generally have sad endings with the traffic on our roadways, so the suburban or country Airedale needs a safe fenced area. While the breed is not at its best in the city, there are exceptions and if there is no garden, a strong lead and lots of walks will have to suffice.

If you admire almost everything about the Airedale, you will still need to go the extra mile to meet character changes as they occur. One that comes to mind is the transition that takes place when the puppy enters adolescence. Perhaps you have known, or raised, teenagers? There are many similarities, but rest assured, it's both easier and briefer to go through this youthful stage with an Airedale! Just keep your sense of humour and continue to be consistently firm in keeping to the house rules—-it will be over in a few months. Airedales are said to reach adulthood at about three years of age. To be truthful, some never really do! Again, it's part of their charm.

The Airedale is self-confident, playful and exuberant. He is a great dog for the right owner who loves an active dog and has the room for such a large companion dog.

25

THE KING OF TERRIERS

On the downside, the Airedale Terrier is what is called 'mouthy,' that is, given to barking loudly and long if not silenced, which is one reason he should not be tied up. Any dog tied up outdoors will initiate a barking scenario which goes like this: Dog barks non-stop. Person shouts at dog to stop (in other words, barks back). Dog barks in response; person barks back, and so on and on, infuriating everyone in earshot. Airedales are social animals and need to be with the family, not left alone without anyone to follow about or to curl up beside. The remedy is a fenced area, regular outdoor play or a nice (preferably long) walk.

The owner of an Airedale Terrier definitely needs a sense of humour; to be fair, firm and consistent; to reward every well-meaning effort with verbal praise and to be generous with treats for jobs well done. Remember always that if you cannot control your Airedale, he will gladly—and instantly—step in and control you. Terriers are all opportunists, always ready and able to move up in the family hierarchy and the Airedale probably tops the list in this skill. From the canine viewpoint, weak leaders cannot be trusted with the safety and survival of the pack, so when we say the Airedale is capable of taking on any job that includes becoming Chairman of the Board. After all, he knows he's the 'King of Terriers'!

However, any dog with such innate versatility and intelligence is not one to submit easily to rote training. He is persistently distracted by sight, sound and scent, whereas most other breeds are governed by only one or two of these three drives. The owner needs to understand this diverse mental energy before beginning to train. Instructors used to contend that terriers in general did not make good pupils, going so far as to label them 'terrible terriers' or 'untrainable terriers.' Lately many enlightened trainers have come to realise it is not the terrier that's the problem, but rather the method of teaching. Positive reinforcement (praise for the right response to a given command) works, whereas harsh verbal and physical corrections for failure do not. This affirmative reasoning extends also to training equipment where the head collar has proven to be a far better choice for terriers than the chain choke collar.

The Airedale is instinctively a protector of his property and his family and his size and strong bark, which exposes large teeth in powerful jaws, make him a formidable foe to the unwary. Only if he senses the need to do so will he attack. Wherever the Airedale is used as a guard dog, he is trained for the job. One hears many more reports of Airedales saving toddlers from drowning or from darting into traffic than stories of Airedale attacks on intruders.

One day two of my husband's business associates came to the house to wait for him. The Airedale greeted both men in a friendly, but formal, manner and lay down between where they were seated and where I sat, seemingly asleep. One of the men partially rose out of his chair to reach an ashtray and the dog's head was over his arm in a flash! No growl, no curled lip, no sign of aggression other than a look and body language that said it all: 'Watch it! I'm on duty here.'

The hereditary factor of gunshyness has been a source of arguments for years among those who hunt their dogs. Unreasonable shyness should be looked upon as a more serious breed fault than houndy ears, bad tail set or a soft coat, all of which may be faulty in show circles but perfectly acceptable in a loveable pet. A steady, friendly outgoing temperament, however, is of paramount importance in the family Airedale, as it should be in a show dog, working dog and obedience dog.

THE AIREDALE AT WORK

In *Cynographia Britannica* (1800) Syndenham Edwards wrote of

Dogs, Dogs, Good for Your Heart!

People usually purchase dogs for companionship, but studies show that dogs can help to improve their owners' health and level of

activity, as well as lower a human's risk of coronary heart disease. Without even realising it, when a person puts time into exercising, grooming and feeding a dog, he also puts more time into his own personal health care. Dog owners establish a more routine schedule for their dogs to follow, which can have positive effects on a human's health. Dogs also teach us patience, offer unconditional love and provide the joy of having a furry friend to pet!.

terriers as a whole, 'As his courage is great, so is his genius extensive; he will trace with the foxhounds, hunt with the beagle, find with the greyhound, or beat with the spaniel. Of wildcats, martens, polecats, weasels and rats, he is the vigilant and determined enemy; he drives the otter from the rocky clefts on the banks of rivers, nor declines combat of a new element.' It is a sad state of affairs that dogs bred to hunt are no longer allowed this pursuit in their native land, but such are the laws today. In America the reverse is happening with more and more people becoming actively involved in breed-specific sporting activities, including carting trials for Bernese Mountain Dogs, sledding races for Huskies and of course terrier trials for Scotties, Dachshunds, etc.

When we speak of working or hunting dogs versus show or breeding stock, we are not referring to different types of Airedale Terriers. There is only one type, the one described in the breed standard. A dog earning hunting, obedience or agility titles may not be up to snuff for the show ring from a 'beauty' standpoint (ears, coat, etc.), but still retains type, and in order to work, it must be sound. Conversely, there is no reason why a show dog could not add other titles to its championship

and many are doing just that.

There are numerous stories, especially in America, of Airedales taking down bears and mountain lions. Their heroics have not gone unnoticed worldwide by the hunting Airedale enthusiasts, nor has that group been reticent to laud the breed's natural accomplishments over those achieved in the show ring! As a result, dogs bred for show, including those that actually are conformation champions, are becoming increasingly involved in field work.

The Airedale's working attributes have gone far beyond anything perceived by the breed's creators. In the early 1900s in America, Walter Lingo began to breed and train Airedales for hunting. Oorang Airedales (he never called them Airedale Terriers) were not AKC registered, ranged in size from 15.91 to 45.36 kgs (35 to 100 lbs), came in any ancestral colour and were without any adherence to type! He advertised them as hunters, but was hardly original in his claim. As Gladys Brown Edwards, noted breeder, author and artist wrote, 'In fact, it is harder to keep an Airedale from hunting than it is to find one reluctant to hunt.'

Will Judy, writing in *Dog Encyclopedia* (Chicago, 1936), raved about the dog's capabilities, including success as a police dog and on the battlefield, as a hunter of wild game (lions and tigers) in Africa, as a retriever in icy waters, as a sled dog in the frozen North, etc. High praise indeed, but he also noted that the Airedale Terrier wears his heart on his sleeve, is sensitive, demands attention and praise, but 'all with a loveable terrier nature.' He was right on the mark!

Before considering the Airedale as a family pet, one must consider the breed's instinctive working traits. Potential owners must realise these are active dogs, not hyperactive dogs, but are working terriers with a will and a need to be given something to do. The alternative is to get into mischief. Small jobs are perfectly acceptable. Such tasks as carrying in the morning paper or toting a basket of tools about the garden qualify as gainful employment, so long as you remember that the dog also needs sufficient physical exercise.

During an off season, show dogs and hunters are trotted alongside a bicycle to keep them in top condition. For the pet, a brisk walk, retrieving a toy over and over again, or perhaps his favourite—a run in the fields adjacent to an irresistible stream or pond—will do nicely. City dogs can make do with similar excursions in the park.

Agility trials are the latest form of 'work' and running the agility course is pure fun for the

The Airedale puppy grows into a fearless, determined animal, capable of undertaking any task set before him.

dogs even if they never go beyond practice sessions. An Airedale is a good companion for the person who jogs every day. Watch the dog's weight if he prefers his dinner bowl and a comfy sofa to walks.

It is difficult to lump all aspects of the Airedale together and say, 'There you have it, that's what the Airedale is like.' Each dog is a complex individual, with attributes and deficiencies derived from his genes, his people and his environment. After all this talk about work, many an owner will cheerfully attest to the fact that their Airedale is merely an oversized lapdog!

My sons taught one of their Airedales to run races with them.

They enjoyed the game until they realised the dog was winning every race with a sudden burst of speed just before reaching the finish line no matter how many times they extended that mark. They switched to football, only to have the dog figure out how to trap the ball inside four firmly planted feet. Good playmates for kids? Intelligent? Playful dogs? Yes, indeed.

The breed is exceptionally good with children but, as with every other breed of dog, that means 'good with good, well-behaved slightly older children.' When the Airedale has been a family member for some time, there should be no problem when a new baby arrives. However, when buying the first family dog, it's best if the children are eight years of age or older.

To sum up the Airedale as a companion, he is a gentle, trustworthy playmate and faithful protector of home and family. At the same time, he's a formidable watchdog. His intelligence is unsurpassed, yet he can be endearingly foolish, a clown to make you laugh or to dispel your tears. He'll give you a look that will warm your heart, and put his chin on your knee just to let you know he's there.

HEALTH CONSIDERATIONS
It's always dangerous to say a breed has few health problems, but the Airedale is so blessed. Apart from worms, which are easily controlled today, and skin conditions due to flea bites or diet (also controllable), the breed enjoys a relatively clean bill of health.

Hip dysplasia (HD), which can occur in any dog, but more often in the large ones, is present in the Airedale and research is underway into its hereditary aspects. Since it is an inherited debilitating disease, the prospective buyer should enquire as to a veterinary surgeon's evaluation of the sire's and dam's hips. There are special tests to detect HD. A dog with the lowest degree of affliction may never show any signs of the disorder. More severe cases result in painful disuse of one or both hind legs and are treated with pain-relieving medication or surgery including the latest in total hip replacement.

Occasionally von Willebrand's disease, which is an inherited coagulation abnormality, occurs in Airedales.

There is growing concern over problems with the immune system, tracing some of it to an over-reaction of the dog's system to the broad use of multiple immunizations. Some breeders are now cutting back on the number and frequency of these shots, but consult your veterinary surgeon for guidance.

The Airedale is especially good with children. Teach your child the responsibilities of ownership so that she respects her puppy and treats him appropriately.

'slightly' or 'moderately' also are used where a specific definition is not key to overall judgement.

The Airedale standard originated in England where it was usual for the writers to be horsemen or stockmen, men who could determine top quality in almost every animal from rabbit to sheep to horses to dogs. For that very reason, the first breed standards for dogs did not declare the obvious: 'four legs and a bark' being left unsaid. The present Kennel Club Airedale standard seen here includes the gait as does the American standard. Both give the desired height, but not weight since the description under 'General Appearance' offers a picture of the desired overall balance and the breed no longer varies in these aspects as it did at the start of its development.

In the 1960s poor front movement in the Airedale had become quite common and judges were forced simply to go with the best of a bad lot, pointing out in their critiques how critical proper movement was in a large working terrier. Breeders got the message and fronts soon improved. The author cites this as a specific

At dog shows, the dogs are measured against the breed standard. The Airedale Terrier who most closely conforms to the breed standard is selected as the winner.

A breed standard is a written blueprint of the perfect specimen for breeders and judges to use in evaluating the essential aspects of the breed described. Its primary concern is to describe conformation in enough detail to include type and soundness allowing one to visualize the dog with some degree of accuracy. Conversely, bland modifiers such as 'fairly,' example of how concerned people can use a breed standard properly.

The Airedale is felt by many to be a 'head' dog. In other words, if the head is not what's wanted in proportions, planes and expression, the dog is thought to lack type and therefore to be of inferior show or breeding quality. The in-depth section on 'Head and Skull' in the standard would lend credence to this viewpoint.

The 'Scale of Points' is no longer a part of the Airedale breed standard, but breeders and judges often refer to it as a reminder of how the founders of the breed wanted the emphasis on the parts of the dog apportioned.

Despite this pattern for perfection, evaluating the Airedale Terrier is subjective. Designated breed faults are faults, but what one person forgives in the whelping box or show ring as a minor imperfection, another person sees as a major defect. One judge is smitten by a fabulous coat, another overlooks a less-than-great coat in favour of a perfect ear-set, but in the end the determination of which dog gets the prize is based on an appraisal of the whole dog.

The standard included here is approved by The Kennel Club, the governing body of the dog world in England, which controls all breed standards and determines when alterations should be instituted.

EXPENSE OF BREEDING

The decision to breed your dog is one that must be considered carefully and researched thoroughly before moving into action. Some people believe that breeding will make their bitch happier or that it is an easy way to make money. Unfortunately, indiscriminate

breeding only worsens the rampant problem of pet overpopulation, as well as putting a considerable dent in your purse. As for the bitch, the entire process from mating through whelping is not an easy one and puts your pet under considerable stress. Last, but not least, consider whether or not you have the means to care for an entire litter of pups. Without a reputation in the field, your attempts to sell the pups may be unsuccessful.

BREEDER'S BLUEPRINT

If you are considering breeding your bitch, it is very important that you are familiar with the breed standard. Reputable breeders breed with the intention of producing dogs that are as close as possible to the standard, and contribute to the advancement of the

breed. Study the standard for both physical appearance and temperament, and make certain your bitch and your chosen stud dog measure up.

THE KENNEL CLUB STANDARD FOR THE AIREDALE TERRIER

General Appearance: Largest of the Terriers, a muscular, active, fairly cobby dog, without suspicion of legginess or undue length of body.

Characteristics: Keen of expression, quick of movement, on the tiptoe of expectation at any movement. Character denoted and shown by expression of eyes, and by carriage of ears and erect tail.

Temperament: Outgoing and confident, friendly, courageous and intelligent. Alert at all times, not aggressive but fearless.

Head and Skull: Skull long and flat, not too broad between ears, and narrowing slightly to eyes. Well balanced, with no apparent difference in length between skull and foreface. Free from wrinkles, with stop hardly visible; cheeks level and free from fullness. Foreface well filled up before eyes, not dish-faced or falling away quickly below eyes, but a delicate chiselling prevents appearance of wedginess or plainness. Upper and lower jaws deep, powerful, strong and muscular, as strength of foreface is greatly desired. No excess development of the jaws to give a rounded or bulging appearance to the cheeks, as 'cheekiness' is undesirable. Lips tight, nose black.

An undesirable head, showing too much stop (dishface) with cheeks too full.

The correct head.

Eyes: Dark in colour, small, not prominent, full of terrier expression, keenness and intelligence. Light or bold eye highly undesirable.

Ears: V-shaped with a side carriage, small but not out of proportion to size of dog. Top line

Incorrect ears; too small and too high.

Correct ears.

closely overlapping lower teeth and set square to the jaws preferable, but vice-like bite acceptable. An overshot or undershot mouth undesirable.

Neck: Clear, muscular, of moderate length and thickness, gradually widening towards shoulders, and free from throatiness.

Forequarters: Shoulders long, well laid back, sloping obliquely, shoulder blades flat. Forelegs perfectly straight, with good bone. Elbows perpendicular to body, working free of sides.

Body: Back short, strong, straight and level, showing no slackness. Loins muscular. Ribs well sprung. In short-coupled and well ribbed-

Correct front.   **Undesirable front; with toes turning out.**

of folded ear slightly above level of skull. Pendulous ears or ears set too high undesirable.

Mouth: Teeth strong. Jaws strong. Scissor bite, i.e. upper teeth

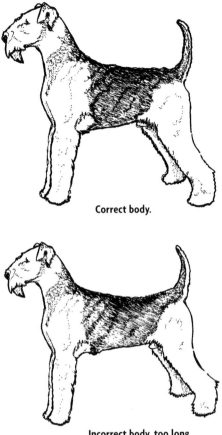

Correct body.

Incorrect body, too long.

Feet: Small, round and compact, with a good depth of pad, well cushioned, and toes moderately arched, turning neither in nor out.

Tail: Set on high and carried gaily, not curled over back. Good strength and substance. Customarily docked. Tip approximately at the same height as top of skull.

Gait/Movement: Legs carried straight forward. Forelegs move freely, parallel to the sides. When approaching, forelegs should form a continuation of the straight line of the front, feet being same distance apart as elbows. Propulsive power is furnished by hindlegs.

Coat: Hard, dense and wiry, not so long as to appear ragged. Lying straight and close, covering body and legs; outer coat hard, wiry and stiff, undercoat shorter and

up dogs there is little space between ribs and hips. When dog is long in couplings some slackness will be shown here. Chest deep (i.e. approximately level with elbows) but not broad.

Hindquarters: Thighs long and powerful with muscular second thigh, stifles well bent, turned neither in nor out. Hocks well let down, parallel with each other when viewed from behind.

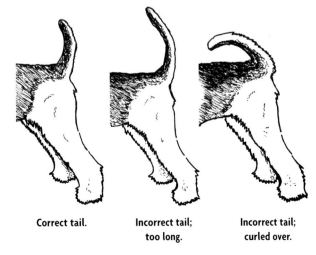

Correct tail.   **Incorrect tail; too long.**   **Incorrect tail; curled over.**

Airedale Terrier

Male and female Airedale Terriers, showing off their distinctly masculine and feminine heads. The female, slightly smaller and more delicate, is in the foreground.

softer. Hardest coats are crinkling or just slightly waved; curly or soft coat highly undesirable.

Colour: Body saddle black or grizzle as is top of the neck and top surface of tail. All other parts tan. Ears often a darker tan, and shading may occur round neck and side of skull. A few white hairs between forelegs acceptable.

Size: Height about 58–61 cms (23–24 ins) for dogs, taken from top of shoulder, and bitches about 56–59 cms (22–23 ins).

Faults: Any departure from the foregoing points should be considered a fault and the seriousness with which the fault should be regarded should be in exact proportion to its degree.

Note: Male animals should have two apparently normal testicles fully descended into the scrotum.

Male and female Airedale Terriers, showing off their distinctly masculine and feminine heads. The female, slightly smaller and more delicate, is in the foreground.

The Airedale Terrier should move freely, with power furnished from the rear quarters. In the show ring, the handler must gait the dog to show its correct movement as described in the standard.

AIREDALE TERRIER

YOU'D LIKE A PUPPY?

All puppies are adorable, including Airedale Terrier puppies, even though at times they may seem unable to manoeuvre all four legs in a recognisable trotting sequence. Like other black and tan breeds, Airedales are born almost entirely black. The tan markings spread over the legs and head as the pup matures and as the puppy coat is replaced by the correct wiry adult coat.

It is a sound investment to buy your puppy from a breeder who has been at it for some time and has a good reputation. A good breeder will select a puppy that will fit well into your family and your lifestyle.

The selection of your Airedale puppy should be a serious undertaking. The colours will change as the dog matures, so do not base your decision on colour pattern.

You'll be given complete information about the pup's life so far, including the quantity and brand of dog food, the puppy's daily routine (rising with the dawn is normal!), and you will be able to ask questions pertaining to your very special puppy.

The litter will have been raised with loving care, which is important whether you're looking for a companion or a show dog. The breeder won't know for many months which pup will be the big winner, so all are given the same attention. When the litter reaches six or eight weeks of age, the breeder will begin to sort out which might be a show prospect and which pet quality. A pet is not a second-rate citizen, but simply does not fit some aspect of the breed standard well enough to be considered for the show ring.

Eight to ten weeks of age is the best time to bring a puppy home because it will have had time to learn canine basics from its dam and littermates. In other words, in that time it begins to learn to be a dog, which is vital to its future interaction with other dogs. It also has started the process of learning how to learn! The next step is for its new family to teach such things as the spoken word, human body language,

what the puppy may and may not do. Every minute of the day you will be teaching the puppy something—whether you mean to or not. It is said that every puppy is a sponge, ready to absorb every single thing in its environment, which is why it is so important to begin teaching right from wrong the moment you collect your little Airedale.

The Airedale puppy's most essential need is you. A puppy left alone too much will have to make its own decisions about everything, and whether to chew the chair legs or to pull over the potted plants is not a decision for a pup to make. Keeping the puppy in a crate when you must leave him alone is a kindness to you both—no harm and a happy homecoming. The crate is also the best bed for an Airedale puppy, with veterinary bedding and a blanket until the need to chew slows down. Dogs like this small, cosy den that is entirely their own. By the way, it is for that reason the crate should never be used in connection with a punishment. It's better to put the dog on a down/stay than to usurp his personal residence. While we're on the subject, feeding the puppy in its crate may inadvertently encourage posses-sive aggression. If there is a

Information . . .

You should not even think about buying a puppy that looks sick, undernourished, overly frightened or nervous. Sometimes a timid puppy will warm up to you after a 30-minute 'let's-get-acquainted' session.

adhere to it religiously.

Children must be taught to respect the puppy's needs and possessions. For their own safety, children must know never to disturb a sleeping dog, not to touch the dog when it is eating, not to be noisy or wild around the puppy and never to tease the dog in any way. Wiggling fingers and playing keepaway with toys are the usual teasing methods children employ. One easy way to make young children understand is to explain that the dog does not have 'hands' and therefore must grab or hold things in its mouth—which is full of needle-sharp teeth.

Depending upon their age, do let the children take some responsibility for the care of the dog, but young ones do forget and will need gentle reminders. Take heart—the dog will also teach the children. One chewed cricket bat or football boot will teach them to pick up and put away their things.

THE ADULT ALTERNATIVE
The choice of an older dog requires more investigation in order to make a happy union. If the dog is from a kennel, the extent of prior socialising and housetraining is important to know. Health background and a current veterinary check-up are

toddler to be concerned about, feed the dog when baby is safely elsewhere.

Airedale puppies are quite easily housetrained (they are intelligent) and only need be taught where. Then it is up to you to set up when, where and how often to take the puppy outside to relieve itself. Set up a by-the-clock schedule and mandatory. Kennel dogs may not be accustomed to normal household noises and the confusion of being among people, furniture, Hoovers, fridge motors that turn on and off by themselves, telephones or doorbells can be alarming to a dog that has never been exposed to them. However, don't be discouraged by this bit of advice because Airedales are very, very good about adjusting to a new environment. Actually, an Airedale that was a kennel dog usually is so delighted to be an 'only child' and the recipient of so much attention, it wouldn't attempt to foul its good fortune.

A good breeder will take back a dog that does not work out provided sufficient time and effort have been put into settling the dog in its new home. An adult dog is a better choice than a puppy for anyone who loves the temperament and personality of an Airedale but couldn't keep up with the pace of a puppy. Some re-training will be necessary until the dog adjusts to your routine. Liken it to your moving to a foreign country where you don't speak the language. Time and a little patience are absolute necessities.

If your choice is a rescue dog, you will be told as much as is known about the dog.

DO YOUR HOMEWORK!
Unfortunately, when a puppy is bought by someone who does not take into consideration the time and attention that dog ownership requires, it is the puppy who suffers when he is either abandoned or placed in a shelter by a frustrated owner. So all of the 'homework' you do in preparation for your pup's arrival will benefit you both. The more informed you are, the more you will know what to expect and the

better equipped you will be to handle the ups and downs of raising a puppy. Hopefully, everyone in the household is willing to do his part in raising and caring for the pup. The anticipation of owning a dog often brings a lot of promises from excited family members: 'I will walk him every day,' 'I will feed him,' 'I will housebreak him,' etc., but these things take time and effort, and promises can easily be forgotten once the novelty of the new pet has worn off.

Puppy Selection

Your selection of a good puppy can be determined by your needs. A show potential or a good pet? It is your choice. Every puppy, however, should be of good temperament.

Although show-quality puppies are bred and raised with emphasis on physical conformation, responsible breeders strive for equally good temperament. Do not buy from a breeder who concentrates solely on physical beauty at the expense of personality.

Those in charge of rescue schemes are usually Airedale Terrier club members and they are very careful to re-home the dogs where they will fit in best.

Fortunately for the breed, the Airedale does not bond for life to one person (although he certainly will go out of his way to make each person in the family think otherwise) and so can adjust readily to new people, a new home and a new routine. The Airedale responds so well to attention, appreciation and affection combined with good-natured re-education that there is seldom a problem in re-homing an older dog.

WHERE TO BEGIN?
If you are convinced that the Airedale Terrier is the ideal dog for you, it's time to learn about where to find a puppy and what to look for. Locating a litter of Airedales should not present a problem for the new owner. You should enquire about breeders in your area who enjoy a good reputation in the breed. You are looking for an established breeder with outstanding dog ethics and a strong commitment to the breed. New owners should have as many questions as they have doubts. An established breeder

DID YOU KNOW?
Your puppy should have a well-fed appearance but not a distended abdomen, which may indicate worms or incorrect feeding, or both. The body should be firm, with a solid feel. The skin of the abdomen should be pale pink and clean, without signs of scratching or rash. Check the hind legs to make certain that dewclaws were removed, if any were present at birth.

is indeed the one to answer your four million questions and make you comfortable with your choice of the Airedale. An established breeder will sell you a puppy at a fair price if, and only if, the breeder determines that you are a suitable, worthy owner of his/her dogs. An established breeder can be relied upon for advice, no matter what time of day or night.

When choosing a breeder, reputation is much more important than convenience of location. Do not be overly impressed by breeders who run brag advertisements in the presses about their stupendous champions and working lines. The real quality breeders are quiet and unassuming. You hear about them at the dog

INSURANCE

Many good breeders will offer you insurance with your new puppy, which is an excellent idea. The first few weeks of insurance will probably be covered free of charge or with only minimal cost, allowing you to take up the policy when this expires. If you own a pet dog, it is sensible to take out such a policy as veterinary fees can be high, although routine vaccinations and boosters are not covered. Look carefully at the many options open to you before deciding which suits you best.

Information . . .

Breeders rarely release puppies until they are eight to ten weeks of age. This is an acceptable age for most breeds of dog, excepting

toy breeds, which are not released until around 12 weeks, given their petite sizes. If a breeder has a puppy that is 12 weeks or more, it is likely well socialised and housetrained. Be sure that it is otherwise healthy before deciding to take it home.

trials and shows, by word of mouth. You may be well advised to avoid the novice who lives only a couple miles away. The local novice breeder, trying so hard to get rid of that first litter of puppies, is more than accommodating and anxious to sell you one. That breeder will charge you as much as any established breeder. The novice breeder isn't going to interrogate you and your family about your intentions with the puppy, the environment and training you can provide, etc. That breeder will be nowhere to be found when your poorly bred, badly

ARE YOU A FIT OWNER?
If the breeder from whom you are buying a puppy asks you a lot of personal questions, do not be insulted. Such a breeder wants to be sure that you will be a fit provider for his puppy.

DOCUMENTATION
Two important documents you will get from the breeder are the pup's pedigree and registration certificate. The breeder should register the litter and each pup with The Kennel Club, and it is necessary for you to have the paperwork if you plan on showing or breeding in the future.

Make sure you know the breeder's intentions on which type of registration he will obtain for the pup. There are limited registrations which may prohibit the dog from being shown, bred or from competing in non-conformation trials such as Working or Agility if the breeder feels that the pup is not of sufficient quality to do so. There is also a type of registration that will permit the dog in non-conformation competition only.

On the reverse side of the registration certificate, the new owner can find the transfer section which must be signed by the breeder.

adjusted four-pawed monster starts to growl and spit up at midnight or eat the family cat!

While health considerations in the Airedale are not nearly as daunting as in most other breeds, socialisation is a breeder concern of immense importance. Since the Airedale's temperament can vary from line to line, socialisation is the first and best way to encourage a proper, stable personality. Whether your choice is an older dog or young puppy, a male or female, socialising the Airedale with people of all ages and with other dogs of all sizes is important for you, for your dog and for your neighbours who would much prefer to know that the large dog next door is friendly.

Choosing a breeder is an important first step in dog ownership. Fortunately, the majority of Airedale breeders are devoted to the breed and its well being. New owners should have little problem finding a reputable breeder who doesn't live on the other side of the country (or in a different country). The Kennel Club is able to recommend breeders of quality Airedales, as can any local all-breed club or Airedale club. Potential owners are encouraged to attend dog shows to see the Airedales in action, to meet owners and handlers firsthand and to get an idea what Airedales look like outside a photographer's lens. Provided you approach the handlers when they are not terribly busy with the dogs, most are more than willing to answer questions, recommend breeders and give advice.

Now that you have contacted and met a breeder or two and made your choice about which breeder is best suited to your needs, it's time to visit the litter. Keep in mind that many top breeders have waiting lists. Sometimes new owners have to wait as long as two years for a puppy. If you are really committed to the breeder whom you've selected, then you will wait (and hope for an early arrival!). If not, you may have to resort to your second or third choice breeder. Don't be too anxious, however. If the breeder doesn't have any waiting list, or any customers, there is probably a good reason. It's no different than visiting a pub with no clientele. The

Your Schedule . . .

If you lead an erratic, unpredictable life, with daily or weekly changes in your work requirements, consider the problems of owning a puppy. The new puppy has to be fed regularly,

socialised (loved, petted, handled, introduced to other people) and, most importantly, allowed to visit outdoors for toilet training. As the dog gets older, it can be more tolerant of deviations in its feeding and toilet relief.

Airedale Terrier

better pubs and restaurants always have a waiting list—and it's usually worth the wait. Besides, isn't a puppy more important than a pint?

Since you are likely to be choosing an Airedale as a pet dog and not a working or show dog, you simply should select a pup that is friendly and attractive. While the basic structure of the breed has little variation, the temperament may present trouble in certain strains. Beware of the shy or overly aggressive puppy: be especially conscious of the nervous

Airedale pup. Don't let sentiment or emotion trap you into buying the runt of the litter.

The choice of gender is definitely up to the individual. Temperament within the breed tends to be individual rather than male vs. female. Some breeders feel the male is more assertive about protecting home and family; others believe the females to be more dominant. I have not found either to be rigid truths. Marking territory, mostly in males, or mood swings in females are modified (although never eliminated) by neutering or spaying. This minor surgery also helps to restrain the adolescent misbehaviour, which can come as a shock to the owner of a previously well-behaved, co-operative puppy.

Unlike in earlier times, commercial breeders are not attracted to the breed. This helps your selection, ensuring that most pups will come from strong lines unencumbered by overbreeding, inbreeding or the countless finicky prejudices that have damaged other show breeds. Given the long history that dogs and humans have, bonding between the two species is natural but must be nurtured. A well-bred, well-socialised Airedale pup wants nothing more than to be near you and please you.

Always check the bite of your selected puppy to be sure that it is neither overshot nor undershot. This may not be too noticeable on a young puppy but it is a fairly common problem with certain lines of Airedales.

COMMITMENT OF OWNERSHIP

After considering all of these factors, you have most likely already made some very important decisions about selecting your puppy. You have chosen an Airedale, which means that you have decided which characteristics you want in a dog and what type of dog will best fit into your family and lifestyle. If you have selected a breeder, you have gone a step further—you have done your research and found a responsible, conscientious person who breeds quality Airedales and who should be a reliable source of help as you and your puppy adjust to life together. If you have observed a litter in action, you have obtained a firsthand look at the dynamics of a puppy 'pack' and, thus, you should learn about each pup's individual personality—perhaps you have even found one that particularly appeals to you.

However, even if you have

FOOD TIPS
The cost of food must also be mentioned. All dogs need a good quality food with an adequate supply of protein to develop their bones and muscles properly. Most dogs are not picky eaters but unless fed properly they can quickly succumb to skin problems.

Puppy Personality

When a litter becomes available to you, choosing a pup out of all those adorable faces will not be an easy task! Sound temperament is of utmost importance, but each pup has its own personality and some may be better suited to you than others. A feisty, independent pup will do well in a home with older children and adults, while quiet, shy puppies will thrive in a home with minimum noise and distractions. Your breeder knows the pups best and should be able to guide you in the right direction.

not yet found the Airedale puppy of your dreams, observing pups will help you learn to recognise certain behaviour and to determine what a pup's behaviour indicates about his temperament. You will be able to pick out which pups are the leaders, which ones are less outgoing, which ones are confident, which ones are shy, playful, friendly, aggressive, etc. Equally as important, you will learn to recognise what a healthy pup should look and act like. All of these things will help you in your search, and when you find the Airedale that was meant for you, you will know it!

Researching your breed, selecting a responsible breeder and observing as many pups as possible are all important steps on the way to dog ownership. It may seem like a lot of effort...and you have not even brought the pup home yet! Remember, though, you cannot be too careful when it comes to deciding on the type of dog you want and finding out about your prospective pup's background. Buying a puppy is not—or should not be—just another whimsical purchase. This is one instance in which you actually do get to choose your own family! You may be thinking that buying a puppy should be fun—it should not be so serious and so much work. Keep in mind that your puppy is not a cuddly stuffed toy or decorative lawn ornament, but a creature that will become a real member of your family. You will come to realise that, while buying a puppy is a pleasurable and exciting endeavour, it is not something to be taken lightly. Relax…the fun will start when the pup comes home!

Always keep in mind that a puppy is nothing more than a baby in a furry disguise…a baby who is virtually helpless in a human world and who trusts his owner for fulfilment of his basic needs for survival. In addition to water and shelter, your pup needs care, protection, guidance and love. If you are not prepared to commit to this, then you are not prepared to own a dog.

Wait a minute, you say. How hard could this be? All of my neighbours own dogs and they seem to be doing just fine. Why should I have to worry about all of this? Well, you should not worry about it; in fact, you will probably find that once your Airedale pup gets used to his new home, he will fall into his place in the family quite naturally. But it never hurts to emphasise the commitment of dog ownership. With

'You Better Shop Around!'

Finding a reputable breeder that sells healthy pups is very important, but make sure that the breeder you choose is not only someone you

respect but also with whom you feel comfortable. Your breeder will be a resource long after you buy your puppy, and you must be able to call with reasonable questions without being made to feel like a pest! If you don't connect on a personal level, investigate some other breeders before making a final decision.

some time and patience, it is really not too difficult to raise a curious and exuberant Airedale pup to be a well-adjusted and well-mannered adult dog—a dog that could be your most loyal friend.

PREPARING PUPPY'S PLACE IN YOUR HOME
Researching your breed and finding a breeder are only two aspects of the 'homework' you will have to do before taking your Airedale puppy home. You will also have to prepare

DO YOUR HOMEWORK!
In order to know whether or not a puppy will fit into your lifestyle, you need to assess his personality. A good way to do this is to interact with his

parents. Your pup inherits not only his appearance but also his personality and temperament from the sire and dam. If the parents are fearful or overly aggressive, these same traits may likely show up in your puppy.

your home and family for the new addition. Much as you would prepare a nursery for a newborn baby, you will need to designate a place in your home that will be the puppy's own. How you prepare your home will depend on how much freedom the dog will be allowed. Whatever you decide, you must ensure that he has a place that he can 'call his own.'

When you bring your new puppy into your home, you are bringing him into what will become his home as well. Obviously, you did not buy a puppy so that he could take over your house, but in order for a puppy to grow into a stable, well-adjusted dog, he has to feel comfortable in his surroundings. Remember, he is leaving the warmth and security of his mother and littermates, as well as the familiarity of the only place he has ever known, so it is important to make his transition as easy as possible. By preparing a place in your home for the puppy, you are making him feel as welcome as possible in a strange new place. It should not take him long to get used to it, but the sudden shock of being transplanted is somewhat traumatic for a young pup. Imagine how a small child would feel in the same situation—that is how your puppy must be feeling. It is up to you to reassure him and to let him know, 'Little chap, you are going to like it here!'

WHAT YOU SHOULD BUY

CRATE

To someone unfamiliar with the use of crates in dog training, it may seem like punishment to shut a dog in a crate, but this is not the case at all. Although all breeders do not advocate crate training, more and more breeders and trainers are

PHOTO COURTESY OF DOSKOCIL.

> **CRATE TRAINING TIPS**
>
> During crate training, you should partition off the section of the crate in which the pup stays. If he is given too big an area, this will hinder your training efforts. Crate training is based on the fact that a dog does not like to soil his sleeping quarters, so it is ineffective to keep a pup in a crate that is so big that he can eliminate in one end and get far enough away from it to sleep. Also, you want to make the crate den-like for the pup. Blankets and a favourite toy will make the crate cosy for the small pup; as he grows, you may want to evict some of his 'roommates' to make more room.
>
> It will take some coaxing at first, but be patient. Given some time to get used to it, your pup will adapt to his new home-within-a-home quite nicely.

recommending crates as a preferred tool for show puppies as well as pet puppies. Crates are not cruel—crates have many humane and highly effective uses in dog care and training. For example, crate training is a very popular and very successful housebreaking method. A crate can keep your

Your pet shop will have a vast array of crates from which you can select the most suitable one for your Airedale Terrier.

wire crate is more open, allowing the air to flow through and affording the dog a view of what is going on around him, while a fibreglass crate is sturdier. Both can double as travel crates, providing protection for the dog. The size of the crate is another thing to consider. Airedale puppies grow rapidly. Some crates are available with a false back that can be moved forward for the ten-week-old puppy and then pushed back as the pup grows. Your breeder will tell you what size you will need for the adult Airedale. Some breeders will lend a 'new puppy' crate (be sure to return it!) so you need only buy the adult size.

BEDDING
Veterinary bedding in the dog's crate will help the dog feel more at home and you may also like to pop in a small blanket. This will take the place of the leaves, twigs, etc., that the pup

dog safe during travel; and, perhaps most importantly, a crate provides your dog with a place of his own in your home. It serves as a 'doggie bedroom' of sorts—your Airedale can curl up in his crate when he wants to sleep or when he just needs a break. Many dogs sleep in their crates overnight. With soft bedding and his favourite toy, a crate becomes a cosy pseudo-den for your dog. Like his ancestors, he too will seek out the comfort and retreat of a den—you just happen to be providing him with something a little more luxurious than his early ancestors enjoyed.

As far as purchasing a crate, the type that you buy is up to you. It will most likely be one of the two most popular types: wire or fibreglass. There are advantages and disadvantages to each type. For example, a

For relaxing around the home, a dog bed is ideal to encourage the dog not to climb onto the furniture.

would use in the wild to make a den; the pup can make his own 'burrow' in the crate. Although your pup is far removed from his den-making ancestors, the denning instinct is still a part of his genetic makeup. Second, until you bring your pup home, he has been sleeping amidst the warmth of his mother and littermates, and while a blanket is not the same as a warm, breathing body, it still provides heat and something with which to snuggle. You will want to wash your pup's bedding frequently in case he has an accident in his crate, and replace or remove any blanket that becomes ragged and starts to fall apart.

TOYS

Toys are a must for dogs of all ages, especially for curious playful pups. Puppies are the 'children' of the dog world, and what child does not love toys? Chew toys provide enjoyment to both dog and owner—your dog will enjoy playing with his favourite toys, while you will enjoy the fact that they distract him from your expensive shoes and leather sofa. Puppies love to chew; in fact, chewing is a physical need for pups as they are teething, and everything looks appetising! The full range of your possessions—from old

Toys, Toys, Toys!

With a big variety of dog toys available, and so many that look like they would be a lot of fun for a dog, be careful in your selection. It is amazing what a set of puppy teeth can do to an

innocent-looking toy, so, obviously, safety is a major consideration. Be sure to choose the most durable products that you can find. Hard nylon bones and toys are a safe bet, and many of them are offered in different scents and flavours that will be sure to capture your dog's attention. It is always fun to play a game of catch with your dog, and there are balls and flying discs that are specially made to withstand dog teeth.

tea towel to Oriental carpet— are fair game in the eyes of a teething pup. Puppies are not all that discerning when it comes to finding something to literally 'sink their teeth into'— everything tastes great!

Airedale Terriers have

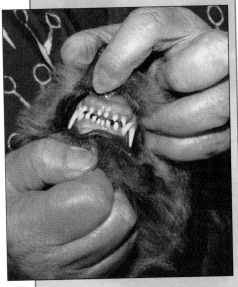

individual dogs will treat every toy as an object to be destroyed, others keep their puppy toys intact well into old age. A boon for the teething puppy is a dampened, knotted towel, cooled in the fridge. It soothes and massages the gums as the pup chews into it.

Squeaky toys are quite popular, but must be avoided for the Airedale. Perhaps a squeaky toy can be used as an aid in training, but not for free play. If a pup 'disembowels' one of these, the small plastic squeaker inside can be dangerous if swallowed. Monitor the condition of all your pup's toys carefully and get rid of any that have been chewed to the point of becoming potentially dangerous.

Be careful of natural bones, which have a tendency to splinter into sharp, dangerous pieces. Also be careful of rawhide, which can turn into pieces that are easy to swallow or into a mushy mess on your carpet.

LEAD
A nylon lead is probably the best option as it is the most resistant to puppy teeth should your pup take a liking to chewing on his lead. Of course, this is a habit that should be nipped in the bud, but if your

grandiose ideas with regard to toys. Bigger really is better! The large rope chew toys are favourites, as are the large fleece toys with squeakers and the large solid rubber ones. These dogs have very strong jaws, so keep a sharp eye on all toys and remove any that are being demolished. Some pup likes to chew on his lead he has a very slim chance of being able to chew through the strong nylon. Nylon leads are also lightweight, which is good for a young Airedale who is just getting used to the idea of walking on a lead. For everyday walking and safety purposes, the nylon lead is a good choice. As your pup grows up and gets used to walking on the lead, you may want to purchase a flexible lead. These leads allow you to extend the length to give the dog a broader area to explore or to shorten the length to keep the dog close to you. Of course there are special leads for training purposes, and specially made leather

All in the terrier family...this Airedale puppy is making the acquaintance of this feisty Fox Terrier pup.

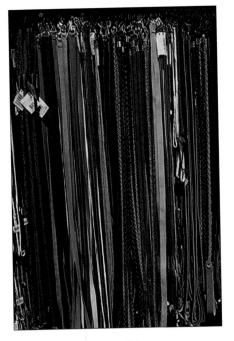

Your pet shop should have a large variety of leads from which you can choose a sturdy but lightweight lead for your Airedale.

but is loose enough so that it will not be uncomfortably tight around the pup's neck. You should be able to fit a finger between the pup and the collar. It may take some time for your pup to get used to wearing the collar, but soon he will not even notice that it is there. Choke collars are made for training, but should only be used by an experienced handler. The headcollar is an excellent tool for teaching the six-month or older puppy to walk nicely beside you. With a slight pull of the lead, the dog's head will turn toward you and you'll have his attention. (Don't forget the rewards!)

harnesses for working Airedales, but these are not necessary for routine walks. A special 6-foot lead will be needed for training, but save a fancy leather collar and lead for the adult Airedale. The puppy will chew through leather in minutes.

COLLAR

Your pup should get used to wearing a collar all the time since you will want to attach his ID tags to it. You have to attach the lead to something! A lightweight nylon collar is a good choice; make sure that it fits snugly enough so that the pup cannot wriggle out of it,

FINANCIAL RESPONSIBILITY

Grooming tools, collars, leashes, dog beds and, of course, toys will be an expense to you when you first obtain your pup, and the cost will continue throughout your dog's lifetime. If your puppy damages or destroys your possessions (as most puppies surely will!) or something belonging to a neighbour, you can calculate additional expense. There is also flea and pest control, which every dog owner faces more than once. You must be able to handle the financial responsibility of owning a dog.

CHOOSING THE PROPER COLLAR

The BUCKLE COLLAR is the standard collar used for everyday purpose. Be sure that you adjust the buckle on growing puppies. Check it every day. It can become too tight overnight! These collars can be made of leather or nylon. Attach your dog's identification tags to this collar.

The CHOKE COLLAR is the usual collar recommended for training. It is constructed of highly polished steel so that it slides easily through the stainless steel loop. The idea is that the dog controls the pressure around its neck and he will stop pulling if the collar becomes uncomfortable. Never leave a choke collar on your dog when not training.

The HALTER is for a trained dog that has to be restrained to prevent running away, chasing a cat and the like. Considered the most humane of all collars, it is frequently used on smaller dogs for which collars are not comfortable.

Bowls come in a variety of shapes, sizes and materials. Choose bowls that are large enough and sturdy enough for your Airedale.

The better quality bowls are made of stainless steel, pottery or heavy plastic.

FOOD AND WATER BOWLS

Your pup will need two bowls, one for food and one for water. You may want two sets of bowls, one for inside and one for outside, depending on where the dog will be fed and where he will be spending most of his time. Stainless steel or sturdy plastic bowls are popular choices. Plastic bowls are more chewable. Dogs tend not to chew on the steel variety, which can be sterilised. It is important to buy sturdy bowls since anything is in danger of being chewed by puppy teeth and you do not want your dog to be constantly chewing apart his bowl (for his safety and for your purse!).

CLEANING SUPPLIES

Until a pup is housetrained you will be doing a lot of cleaning. Accidents will occur, which is okay in the beginning because the puppy does not know any better. All you can do is be prepared to clean up any

PHOTO COURTESY OF MIKKI PET PRODUCTS.

'accidents.' Old rags, towels, newspapers and a safe disinfectant are good to have on hand.

BEYOND THE BASICS

The items previously discussed are the bare necessities. You will find out what else you need as you go along—grooming supplies, flea/tick protection, baby gates to partition a room, etc. These things will vary depending on your situation but it is important that you have everything you need to feed and make your Airedale comfortable in his first few days at home.

PUPPY-PROOFING YOUR HOME

Aside from making sure that your Airedale Terrier will be comfortable in your home, you also have to make sure that your home is safe for your Airedale. This means taking

Natural Toxins

Examine your grass and garden landscaping before bringing your puppy home. Many varieties of plants have leaves, stems or flowers

that are toxic if ingested, and you can depend on a curious puppy to investigate them. Ask your vet for information on poisonous plants or research them at your library.

PUPPY-PROOFING

Thoroughly puppy-proof your house before bringing your puppy home. Never use roach or rodent poisons in any area accessible to the puppy. Avoid the use of toilet cleaners. Most dogs are born with 'toilet sonar' and will take a drink if the lid is left open. Also keep the rubbish secured and out of reach.

precautions that your pup will not get into anything he should not get into and that there is nothing within his reach that may harm him should he sniff it, chew it, inspect it, etc. This probably seems obvious since, while you are primarily concerned with your pup's safety, at the same time you do not want your belongings to be ruined. Breakables should be placed out of reach if your dog is to have full run of the house. If he is to be limited to certain places within the house, keep

CHEMICAL TOXINS

Scour your garage for potential puppy dangers. Remove weed killers, pesticides and antifreeze materials. Antifreeze is highly toxic and even a few drops can kill an adult dog. The sweet taste attracts the animal, who will quickly consume it from the floor or curbside.

any potentially dangerous items in the 'off-limits' areas. An electrical cord can pose a danger should the puppy decide to taste it—and who is going to convince a pup that it would not make a great chew toy? Cords should be fastened tightly against the wall. If your dog is going to spend time in a crate, make sure that there is nothing near his crate that he can reach if he sticks his curious little nose or paws through the openings. Just as you would with a child, keep all household cleaners and chemicals where the pup cannot get to them.

It is also important to make sure that the outside of your home is safe. Of course your puppy should never be unsupervised, but a pup let loose in the garden will want to run and explore, and he should

be granted that freedom. Do not let a fence give you a false sense of security; you would be surprised how crafty (and persistent) a dog can be in working out how to dig under and squeeze his way through small holes, or to jump or climb over a fence. The remedy is to make the fence high enough so that it really is impossible for your dog to get over it (about 3 metres should suffice), and well embedded into the ground. Be sure to repair or secure any gaps in the fence. Check the fence periodically to ensure that it is in good shape and make repairs as needed; a very determined pup may return to the same spot to 'work on it' until he is able to get through.

FIRST TRIP TO THE VET
You have picked out your puppy, and your home and family are ready. Now all you have to do is collect your Airedale from the breeder and the fun begins, right? Well...not so fast. Something else you need to prepare is your pup's first trip to the veterinary surgeon. Perhaps the breeder can recommend someone in the area that specialises in Airedales, or maybe you know some other Airedale owners who can suggest a good vet. Either way, you should have an

appointment arranged for your pup before you pick him up.

The pup's first visit will consist of an overall examination to make sure that the pup does not have any problems that are not apparent to the eye. The veterinary surgeon will also set up a schedule for the pup's vaccinations; the breeder will inform you of which ones the pup has already received and the vet can continue from there.

INTRODUCTION TO THE FAMILY

Everyone in the house will be excited about the puppy coming home and will want to pet him and play with him, but it is best to make the introduction low-key so as not to overwhelm the puppy. He is apprehensive already. It is the first time he has been separated from his mother and the breeder, and the ride to your home is likely to be the first time he has been in a car. The last thing you want to do is smother him, as this will only frighten him further. This is not to say that human contact is not extremely necessary at this stage, because this is the time when a connection between the pup and his human family is formed. Gentle petting and soothing words should help console him, as well as just

DID YOU KNOW?

Taking your dog from the breeder to your home in a car can be a very uncomfortable experience for both of you. The puppy will have been taken from his warm, friendly, safe environ-

ment and brought into a strange new environment. An environment that moves! Be prepared for loose bowels, urination, crying, whining and even fear biting. With proper love and encouragement when you arrive home, the stress of the trip should quickly disappear.

putting him down and letting him explore on his own (under your watchful eye, of course).

The pup may approach the family members or may busy himself with exploring for a while. Gradually, each person should spend some time with the pup, one at a time, crouching down to get as close to the pup's level as possible

and letting him sniff their hands and petting him gently. He definitely needs human attention and he needs to be touched—this is how to form an immediate bond. Just remember that the pup is experiencing a lot of things for the first time, at the same time. There are new people, new noises, new smells, and new things to investigate: so be gentle, be affectionate, and be as comforting as you can be.

YOUR PUP'S FIRST NIGHT HOME

You have travelled home with your new charge safely in his crate. He's been to the vet for a thorough check-up, he's been weighed, his papers examined; perhaps he's even been vaccinated and wormed as well. He's met the family, licked the whole family, including the excited children and the less-than-happy cat. He's explored his area, his new bed, the garden and anywhere else he's been permitted. He's eaten his first meal at home and relieved himself in the proper place. He's heard lots of new sounds, smelled new friends and seen more of the outside world than ever before.

That was just the first day! He's worn out and is ready for bed...or so you think!

It's puppy's first night and you are ready to say 'Good night'—keep in mind that this is puppy's first night ever to be sleeping alone. His dam and littermates are no longer at paw's length and he's a bit scared, cold and lonely. Be reassuring to your new family member. This is not the time to spoil him and give in to his inevitable whining.

Puppies whine to let the others know where they are and hopefully to get company out of it. Place your pup in his new bed or crate in his room and close the door. Mercifully, he may fall asleep without a peep. If the inevitable occurs, ignore the whining: he is fine. Be strong and keep his interest in mind. Do not allow your heart to become guilty and visit the pup. He will fall asleep.

Many breeders recommend placing a piece of bedding from his former home in his new bed so that he recognises the scent of his littermates. Others still advise placing a hot water bottle in his bed for warmth. This latter may be a good idea provided the pup doesn't attempt to suckle—he'll get good and wet and may not fall asleep so fast.

Puppy's first night can be somewhat stressful for the pup and his new family. Remember that you are setting the tone of nighttime at your house. Unless you want to play with your pup every evening at 10 p.m., midnight and 2 a.m., don't initiate the habit. Your family will thank you, and so will your pup!

Socialisation

Thorough socialisation includes not only meeting new people but also being introduced to new experiences such as riding in the car, having his coat brushed, hearing the television, walking in a crowd—the list is endless. The more your pup experiences, and the more positive the experiences are, the less of a shock and the less scary it will be for your pup to encounter new things.

PREVENTING PUPPY PROBLEMS

SOCIALISATION

Now that you have done all of the preparatory work and have helped your pup get accustomed to his new home and family, it is about time for you to have some fun! Socialising your Airedale pup gives you the opportunity to show off eight-to-ten-week period, also known as the fear period. The interaction he receives during this time should be gentle and reassuring. Lack of socialisation can manifest itself in fear and aggression as the dog grows up. He needs lots of human contact, affection, handling and exposure to other animals.

Once your pup has received his necessary vaccinations, feel free to take him out and about (on his lead, of course). Walk him around the neighbourhood, take him on your daily errands, let people pet him, let him meet other dogs and pets, etc. Puppies do not have to try to make friends; there will be no shortage of people who will want to introduce themselves. Just make sure that you carefully supervise each meeting. If the neighbourhood children want to say hello, for example, that is great—children and pups most often make great companions. Sometimes an excited child can unintention-ally handle a pup too roughly, or an overzealous pup can playfully nip a little too hard. You want to make socialisation experiences positive ones. What a pup learns during this very formative stage will impact his attitude toward future encounters. You want your dog to be comfortable around everyone. A pup that

your new friend, and your pup gets to reap the benefits of being an adorable furry creature that people will want to pet and, in general, think is absolutely precious!

Besides getting to know his new family, your puppy should be exposed to other people, animals and situations, but of course he must not come into close contact with dogs you don't know well until his course of injections is fully complete. This will help him become well adjusted as he grows up and less prone to being timid or fearful of the new things he will encounter. Your pup's socialisation began at the breeder's but now it is your responsibility to continue it. The socialisation he receives up until the age of 12 weeks is the most critical, as this is the time when he forms his impres-sions of the outside world. Be especially careful during the has a bad experience with a child may grow up to be a dog that is shy around or aggressive toward children.

CONSISTENCY IN TRAINING
Dogs, being pack animals, naturally need a leader, or else they try to establish dominance in their packs. When you bring a dog into your family, the choice of who becomes the leader and who becomes the 'pack' is entirely up to you! Your pup's intuitive quest for dominance, coupled with the fact that it is nearly impossible to look at an adorable Airedale pup, with his 'puppy-dog' eyes and his too-big-for his-head-still-floppy ears, and not cave in, give the pup almost an unfair advantage in getting the upper hand! A pup will definitely test the waters to see what he can and cannot do. Do not give in to those pleading eyes—stand your ground when it comes to disciplining the pup and make sure that all family members do the same. It will only confuse the pup when Mother tells him to get off the sofa when he is used to sitting up there with Father to watch the nightly news. Avoid discrepancies by having all members of the household decide on the rules before the pup even comes home...and be consistent in enforcing them!

DID YOU KNOW?
It will take at least two weeks for your puppy to become accustomed to his new surroundings. Give him lots of love, attention, handling, frequent opportunities to relieve himself, a diet he likes to eat and a place he can call his own.

Early training shapes the dog's personality, so you cannot be unclear in what you expect.

COMMON PUPPY PROBLEMS
The best way to prevent puppy problems is to be proactive in stopping an undesirable behaviour as soon as it starts. The old saying 'You can't teach an old dog new tricks' does not necessarily hold true, but it is true that it is much easier to discourage bad behaviour in a young developing pup than to wait until the pup's bad behaviour becomes the adult dog's bad habit. There are some problems that are especially prevalent in puppies as they develop.

CHEWING TIPS

Chewing goes hand in hand with nipping in the sense that a teething puppy is always looking for a way to soothe his aching gums. In this case, instead of chewing on you, he may have taken a liking to your favourite shoe or something else which he should not be chewing. Again, realise that this is a normal canine behaviour that does not need to be discouraged, only redirected. Your pup just needs to be taught what is acceptable to

chew on and what is off limits. Consistently tell him NO when you catch him chewing on something forbidden and give him a chew toy. Conversely, praise him when you catch him chewing on something appropriate. In this way you are discouraging the inappropriate behaviour and reinforcing the desired behaviour. The puppy chewing should stop after his adult teeth have come in, but an adult dog continues to chew for various reasons—perhaps because he is bored, perhaps to relieve tension or perhaps he just likes to chew. That is why it is important to redirect his chewing when he is still young.

NIPPING

As puppies start to teethe, they feel the need to sink their teeth into anything available...unfortunately that includes your fingers, arms, hair, and toes. You may find this behaviour cute for the first five seconds...until you feel just how sharp those puppy teeth are. This is something you want to discourage immediately and consistently with a firm 'No!' (or whatever number of firm 'No's' it takes for him to understand that you mean business). Then replace your finger with an appropriate chew toy. While this behaviour is merely annoying when the dog is young, it can become dangerous as your Airedale's adult teeth grow in and his jaws develop, and he continues to think it is okay to gnaw on human appendages. Your Airedale does not mean any harm with a friendly nip, but he also does not know his own strength.

TRAINING TIP

Training your puppy takes much patience and can be frustrating at times, but you should see results from your efforts. If you have a puppy that seems untrainable, take him to a trainer or behaviourist. The dog may have a personality problem that requires the help of a professional, or perhaps you need help in learning how to train your dog.

CRYING

Your pup will often cry, whine, whimper, howl or make some type of commotion when he is left alone. This is basically his way of calling out for attention to make sure that you know he is there and that you have not forgotten about him. He feels insecure when he is left alone, when you are out of the house and he is in his crate or when you are in another part of the house and he cannot see you. The noise he is making is an expression of the anxiety he feels at being alone, so he needs to be taught that being alone is okay. You are not actually training the dog to stop making noise, you are training him to feel comfortable when he is alone and thus removing the need for him to make the noise. This is where the crate comes in handy. You want to know that he

NO CHOCOLATE!
Use treats to bribe your dog into a desired behaviour. Try small pieces of hard cheese or freeze-dried liver. Never offer chocolate as it has toxic qualities for dogs.

DID YOU KNOW?
The majority of problems that are commonly seen in young pups will disappear as your dog gets older. However, how you deal with problems when he is young will determine how he reacts to discipline as an adult dog. It is important to establish who is boss (hopefully it will be you!) right away when you are first bonding with your dog. This bond will set the tone for the rest of your life together.

is safe when you are not there to supervise, and you know that he will be safe in his crate rather than roaming freely about the house. In order for the pup to stay in his crate without making a fuss, he needs to be comfortable in his crate. On that note, it is extremely important that the crate is never used as a form of punishment, or the pup will have a negative association with the crate.

Accustom the pup to the crate in short, gradually increasing time intervals in which you put him in the crate, maybe with a treat, and stay in the room with him. If he cries or makes a fuss, do not go to him, but stay in his sight. Gradually he will realise that staying in his crate is all right without your help, and it will not be so traumatic for him when you are not around. You may want to leave the radio on softly when you leave the house; the sound of human voices may be comforting to him.

DIETARY AND FEEDING CONSIDERATIONS

Today the choices of food for your Airedale Terrier are many and varied. There are simply dozens of brands of food in all sorts of flavours and textures, ranging from puppy diets to those for seniors. There are even hypoallergenic and low-calorie diets available. Because your Airedale Terrier's food has a bearing on coat, health and temperament, it is essential that the most suitable diet is selected

FOOD STORAGE TIP

You must store your dried dog food carefully. Open packages of dog food quickly lose their vitamin value, usually within 90 days of being opened. Mould spores and vermin could also contaminate the food.

TESTING FOR PROPER DIET

A good test for proper diet is the colour, odour and firmness of your dog's stool. A healthy dog usually produces three semi-hard stools per day. The stools should have no unpleasant odour. They should be the same colour from excretion to excretion.

for a Airedale Terrier of his age. It is fair to say, however, that even dedicated owners can be somewhat perplexed by the enormous range of foods available. Only understanding what is best for your dog will help you reach a valued decision.

Dog foods are produced in three basic types: dried, semi-moist and tinned. Dried foods are useful for the cost-conscious for overall they tend to be less expensive than semi-moist or tinned. These contain the least fat and the most preservatives. In general tinned foods are made up of 60–70 percent water, while semi-moist ones often contain so much sugar that they are perhaps the least preferred by owners, even though their dogs seem to like them.

When selecting your dog's diet, three stages of development must be considered: the puppy stage, adult stage and the senior or veteran stage.

PUPPY STAGE

Puppies instinctively want to suck milk from their mother's teats and a normal puppy will exhibit this behaviour from just a few moments following birth. If puppies do not attempt to suckle within the first half-hour or so, they should be encouraged to do so by placing them on the nipples, having selected ones with plenty of milk. This early milk supply is important in providing colostrum to protect the puppies during the first eight to ten weeks of their lives. Although a mother's milk is much better than any milk formula, despite there being some excellent ones available, if the puppies do not feed you will have to feed them yourself. For those with less experience, advice from a veterinary surgeon is important so that you feed not only the right quantity of milk but that of correct quality, fed at suitably frequent intervals, usually every two hours during the first few days of life.

Puppies should be allowed

Food Preference

Selecting the best dried dog food is difficult. There is no majority consensus among veterinary scientists as to the value of nutrient analyses (protein, fat, fibre, moisture, ash, cholesterol, minerals, etc.). All agree that feeding trials are what matters, but you also have to consider the individual dog. Its weight, age, activity and what pleases its taste, all must

be considered. It is probably best to take the advice of your veterinary surgeon. Every dog's dietary requirements vary, even during the lifetime of a particular dog.

If your dog is fed a good dried food, it does not require supplements of meat or vegetables. Dogs do appreciate a little variety in their diets so you may choose to stay with the same brand, but vary the flavour. Alternatively you may wish to add a little flavoured stock to give a difference to the taste.

TIPPING THE SCALES

Good nutrition is vital to your dog's health, but many people end up over-feeding or giving unnecessary supplements. Here are some common doggie diet don'ts:

• Adding milk, yoghurt and cheese to your dog's diet may seem like a good idea for coat and skin care, but dairy products are very fattening and can cause indigestion.

• Diets high in fat will not cause heart attacks in dogs but will certainly cause your dog to gain weight.

• Most importantly, don't assume your dog will simply stop eating once he doesn't need any more food. Given the chance, he will eat you out of house and home!

year of life. Veterinary surgeons are usually able to offer advice in this regard and, although the frequency of meals will have been reduced over time, only when a young dog has reached the age of about 18 months should an adult diet be fed.

Puppy and junior diets should be well balanced for the needs of your dog, so that except in certain circumstances additional vitamins, minerals and proteins will not be required.

ADULT DIETS

A dog is considered an adult when it has stopped growing, so

to nurse from their mothers for about the first six weeks, although from the third or fourth week you will have begun to introduce small portions of suitable solid food. Most breeders like to introduce alternate milk and meat meals initially, building up to weaning time.

By the time the puppies are seven or a maximum of eight weeks old, they should be fully weaned and fed solely on a proprietary puppy food. Selection of the most suitable, good-quality diet at this time is essential for a puppy's fastest growth rate is during the first

GRAIN-BASED DIETS

Some less expensive dog foods are based on grains and other plant proteins. While these products may appear to be attractively priced, many breeders prefer a diet based on animal proteins and believe that they are more conducive to your dog's health. Many grain-based diets rely on soy protein that may cause flatulence (passing gas).

There are many cases, however, when your dog might require a special diet. These special requirements should only be recommended by your veterinary surgeon.

The single most important ingredient of your Airedale's health is his diet. Consult your veterinary surgeon and breeder about the best diet for your Airedale.

in general the diet of an Airedale Terrier can be changed to an adult one at about 10 to 12 months of age. Again you should rely upon your veterinary surgeon or dietary specialist to recommend an acceptable maintenance diet. Major dog food manufacturers specialise in this type of food, and it is just necessary for you to select the one best suited to your dog's needs. Active dogs may have different requirements than sedate dogs.

SENIOR DIETS

As dogs get older, their metabolism changes. The older dog usually exercises less, moves more slowly and sleeps more. This change in lifestyle and physiological performance requires a change in diet. Since these changes take place slowly, they might not be recognisable. What is easily recognisable is weight gain. By continuing to feed your dog an adult-maintenance diet when it is slowing down metabolically, your dog

73

will gain weight. Obesity in an older dog compounds the health problems that already accompany old age.

As your dog gets older, few of his organs function up to par. The kidneys slow down and the intestines become less efficient. These age-related factors are best handled with a change in diet and a change in feeding schedule to give smaller portions that are more easily digested.

There is no single best diet for every older dog. While many dogs do well on light or senior diets, other dogs do better on puppy diets or other special premium diets such as lamb and rice. Be sensitive to your senior Airedale Terrier's diet and this will help control other problems that may arise with your old friend.

WATER

Just as your dog needs proper nutrition from his food, water is

Fatty Risks

Any dog of any breed can suffer from obesity. Studies show that nearly 30 percent of our dogs are overweight, primarily from high caloric intake and low energy expenditure. The hound and gundog breeds are the most likely affected, and females are at a greater risk of obesity than males. Pet dogs that are neutered are twice as prone to obesity as intact, whole dogs.

Regardless of breed, your dog should have a visible 'waist' behind his rib cage and in front of the hind legs. There should be no fatty deposits on his hips or over his rump, and his abdomen should not be extended.

Veterinary specialists link obesity with respiratory problems, cardiac disease and liver dysfunction as well as low sperm count and abnormal oestrous cycles in breeding animals. Other complications include musculoskeletal disease (including arthritis), decreased immune competence, diabetes mellitus, hypothyroidism, pancreatitis and dermatosis. Other studies have indicated that excess fat leads to heat stress, as obese dogs cannot regulate their body temperatures as well as normal-weight dogs.

Don't be discouraged if you discover that your dog has a heart problem or a complicated neurological condition requiring special attention. It is possible to tend to his special medical needs. Veterinary specialists focus on areas such as cardiology, neurology and oncology. Veterinary medical associations require rigorous training and experience before granting certification in a speciality. Consulting a specialist may offer you greater peace of mind when seeking treatment for your dog.

What are you feeding your dog?

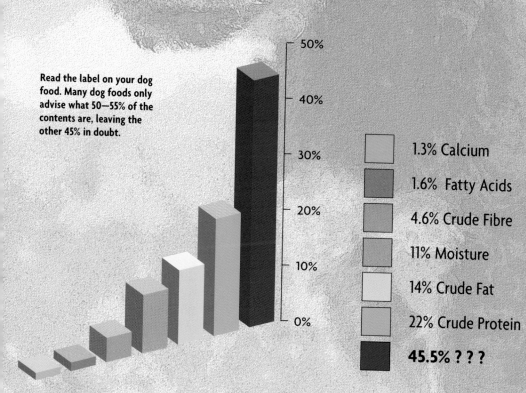

Read the label on your dog food. Many dog foods only advise what 50—55% of the contents are, leaving the other 45% in doubt.

- 1.3% Calcium
- 1.6% Fatty Acids
- 4.6% Crude Fibre
- 11% Moisture
- 14% Crude Fat
- 22% Crude Protein
- **45.5% ? ? ?**

Feeding Tips

Dog food must be at room temperature, neither too hot nor too cold. Fresh water, changed daily and served in a clean bowl, is mandatory, especially when feeding dried food.

Never feed your dog from the table while you are eating. Never feed your dog left-overs from your own meal. They usually contain too much fat and too much seasoning.

Dogs must chew their food. Hard pellets are excellent; soups and slurries are to be avoided.

Don't add leftovers or any extras to normal dog food. The normal food is usually balanced and adding something extra destroys the balance.

Except for age-related changes, dogs do not require dietary variations. They can be fed the same diet, day after day, without their becoming ill.

an essential 'nutrient' as well. Water keeps the dog's body properly hydrated and promotes normal function of the body's systems. During housebreaking it is necessary to keep an eye on how much water your Airedale Terrier is drinking, but once he is reliably trained he should have access to clean fresh water at all times. Make sure that the dog's water bowl is clean, and change the water often, making sure that water is always available for your dog, especially if you feed dried food.

EXERCISE

All dogs require some form of exercise, regardless of breed. A sedentary lifestyle is as harmful to a dog as it is to a person. The Airedale Terrier is an active breed—not a hyperactive breed—that craves stimulation, enjoys exercise and must be made to feel a part of the family's activities. What? No family outings? The Airedale will find some for you and

DO DOGS HAVE TASTE BUDS?

Watching a dog 'wolf' or gobble his food, seemingly without chewing, leads an owner to wonder whether their dogs can taste anything. Yes, dogs have taste buds, with sensory perception of sweet, salty and sour. Puppies are born with fully mature taste buds.

yours. A hike in the wood, a walk in the park and a run on the beach are all in the active Airedale's repertory of fun. Certainly, on a daily basis, letting the dog run free in the garden under your supervision is a must for the Airedale Terrier. Airedales are highly skilled seekers of fun and are blest with many talents, including swimming, hunting, climbing, jogging, etc. No owner of a happy Airedale can be characterised as 'lazy,' unless he's

'DOES THIS COLLAR MAKE ME LOOK FAT?'

While humans may obsess about how they look and how trim their bodies are, many people believe that extra weight on their dogs is a good thing. The truth is, pets should not be over- or under-weight, as both can lead to or signal sickness. In order to tell how fit your pet is, run your hands over his ribs. Are his ribs buried under a layer of fat or are they sticking out considerably? If your pet is within his normal weight range, you should be able to feel the ribs easily. If you stand above him, the outline of his body should resemble an hourglass. Some breeds do tend to be leaner; while some are a bit stockier, but making sure your dog is the right weight for his breed will certainly contribute to his good health.

CHANGE IN DIET

As your dog's caretaker, you know the importance of keeping his diet consistent, but sometimes when you run out of food or if you're on holiday, you have to make a change quickly. Some dogs will experience digestive

problems but most will not. If you are planning on changing your dog's menu, do so gradually to ensure that your dog will not have any problems. Over a period of four to five days, slowly add some new food to your dog's old food, increasing the percentage of new food each day.

Airedale Terrier

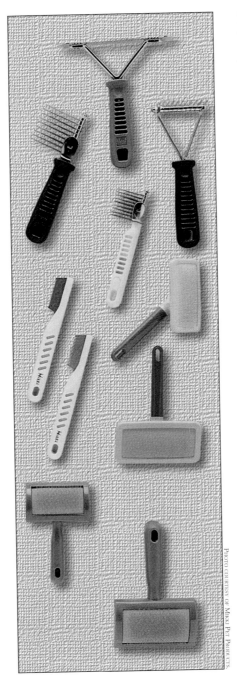

PHOTO COURTESY OF MIKKI PET PRODUCTS.

hired a manservant or 'dog walker' to exercise his Airedale. (Wouldn't that spoil the fun of being an Airedale's main human!? Yes, indeedy.)

Bear in mind that an overweight dog should never be suddenly over-exercised; instead he should be allowed to increase exercise slowly. Not only is exercise essential to keep the dog's body fit, it is essential to his mental well being. A bored dog will find something to do, which often manifests itself in some type of destructive behaviour. In this sense, it is essential for the owner's mental well-being as well!

GROOMING EQUIPMENT

How much grooming equipment you purchase will depend on how much grooming you are going to do. Here are some basics:

- Stiff bristle brush
- Stripping knife
- Raking knife
- Terrier palm pad
- Slicker brush
- Metal comb
- Scissors
- Blaster
- Rubber mat
- Dog shampoo
- Spray hose attachment
- Ear cleaner
- Cotton wipes
- Towels
- Nail clippers

GROOMING

Begin with brief daily grooming sessions—five minutes is a long time to a puppy. Put the puppy on a non-skid pad on a table. A grooming table with a grooming arm and noose (to keep the pup facing forward), or just the arm and noose that can be screwed onto any table or workbench, are worthwhile 10- to 12-year investments. The important thing is to get the pup up off the ground. The ground, be it

DRINK, DRANK, DRUNK— MAKE IT A DOUBLE

In both humans and dogs, as well as most living organisms, water forms the major part of nearly every body tissue. Naturally, we take water for granted, but without it, life as we know it would cease.

For dogs, water is needed to keep their bodies functioning biochemically. Additionally, water is needed to replace the water lost while panting. Unlike humans who are able to sweat to dissipate heat, dogs must pant to cool down, thereby losing the vital water from their bodies needed to regulate their body temperatures. Humans lose electrolyte-containing products and other body-fluid components through sweating; dogs do not lose anything except water.

Water is essential always, but especially so when the weather is hot or humid or when your dog is exercising or working vigorously.

indoors or out, is his turf. By putting him on a table, you've got him at a slight disadvantage and therefore it's easier for you to maintain control.

At first, keep the brushing and combing sessions short and not too intense. Remember you are asking a terrier to stand still. It's not their forte. A stiff-bristle brush is good for the puppy and adult coat and all hair is brushed in the direction in which it grows. Begin to introduce the puppy to the stripping knife, at first merely combing through the coat being very careful not to scratch the

Your Airedale puppy will welcome a nice long walk on the weekend or a hike in the woods. Airedales seek fun in everything they do.

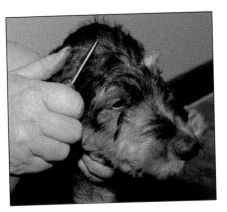

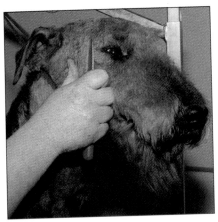

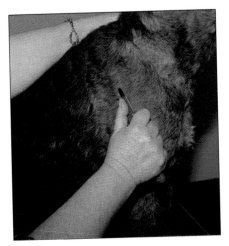

Stripping the Airedale Terrier requires proper instruction and should begin at puppyhood. Discuss coat care with your breeder, Airedale acquaintances or other terrier types.

skin. The easiest hairs to strip from the puppy (actually using the knife or thumb and forefinger) are those on the top of the head and ears.

As the puppy matures, you'll also need a metal comb with both wide and narrow teeth and a pair of scissors for trimming hair between the pads and anywhere else that needs a bit of tidying up. These dogs don't cast coat, so you have to remove the dead hair. A special raking knife will remove it as well as excess undercoat. Be careful not to scratch skin, which will make your dog forever fearful of being groomed.

The adult coat requires more serious grooming, especially on the head to keep that neat rectangular shape. Keeping the hair sparse on the shoulders also helps the dog look tidy and trim. Note that the knife is held with only the tips of a few hairs at a time being lifted by the thumb against the knife, then pulled firmly (with a stiff wrist) in the direction the hair grows.

A 'terrier palm pad' (or dolling-up pad) is best for the adult furnishings on legs and face. On the legs, the pad is placed into the furnishings, brushed in a circular motion once or twice and lifted out. This makes the leg hair stand out so it can be shaped by pulling out (with fingers) any hairs that are beyond the desired cylindrical shape of the front legs and the curves of the hindquarters.

TRIMMING

The Airedale Terrier is a 'trimmed' breed, meaning the pictures you see of gorgeous show dogs represent hours of grooming. If you are clever with your hands, you might want to take lessons in hand-stripping. It also requires a great deal of patience. Pulling the hair doesn't hurt the dog if it is done properly. If you are not ready for this kind of grooming, the alternative is to use clippers but, again, get a few lessons first. If neither one has any appeal, seek a professional groomer. Since the Airedale does not cast its old coat, he will soon become a woolly-bully if not kept properly trimmed. Apart from lacking any semblance of a dignified appearance, the dog's coat will mat, causing discomfort and irritated skin.

BATHING

Brushing the Airedale's soft woolly undercoat and the harsh wire coat on top will get rid of most dirt, twigs and other debris, so bathing is only needed if your dog gets into something it shouldn't—mud perhaps. Leg and face furnishings require more frequent brushing,

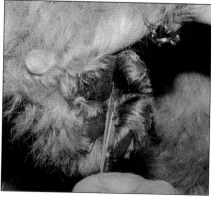

There are special rakes, combs and similar devices with which to groom your puppy.

The hair growing on the bottom of the feet should be scissored.

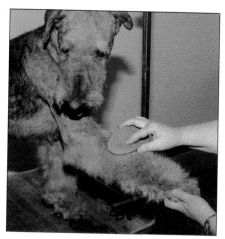

There are many types of palm pad brushes with which to groom the legs of the Airedale.

combing and possibly more shampooing than the entire dog.

Dogs do not need to be bathed as often as humans, but bathing is needed for healthy skin and a healthy, shiny coat. Again, like most anything, if you accustom your pup to being bathed as a puppy, it will be second nature by the time he grows up. You want your dog to be at ease in the bath or else it could end up a wet, soapy, messy ordeal for both of you!

Make certain that your dog has a good non-slip surface to stand on. After brushing, combing and raking, wet the dog through to skin with warm water. Begin by wetting the dog's coat. A shower or hose attachment is necessary

BATHING TIP

The use of human soap products like shampoo, bubble bath and hand soap can be damaging to a dog's coat and skin. Human products are too strong and remove the protective oils coating the dog's hair and skin (making him water-resistant). Use only shampoo made especially for dogs and you may like to use a medicated shampoo, which will always help to keep external parasites at bay.

for thoroughly wetting and rinsing the coat. Check the water temperature to make sure that it is neither too hot nor too cold.

Next, apply shampoo to the dog's coat and work it into a good lather. You should purchase a shampoo that is made for dogs. Do not use a product made for human hair. Wash the head last; you do not want shampoo to drip into the dog's eyes while you are washing the rest of his body. Work the shampoo all the way down to the skin. You can use this opportunity to check the skin for any bumps, bites or other abnormalities. Do not neglect any area of the body—get all of the hard-to-reach places.

Once the dog has been thoroughly shampooed, he requires an equally thorough

BATHING TIP

Once you are sure that the dog is thoroughly rinsed, squeeze the excess water out of the coat with your hand and dry him with a heavy towel. You may choose to use a blaster on his coat or just let it dry naturally. In cold weather, never allow your dog outside with a wet coat.

There are 'dry bath' products on the market, which are sprays and powders intended for spot cleaning, that can be used between regular baths, if necessary. They are not substitutes for regular baths, but they are easy to use for touch-ups as they do not require rinsing.

rinsing. Rinse thoroughly. Then rinse once more. Leaving any soap residue can lead to dry itchy skin problems. Protect his eyes from the shampoo by shielding them with your hand and directing the flow of water in the opposite direction. You should also avoid getting water in the ear canal. Be prepared for your dog to shake out his coat—you might want to stand back, but make sure you have a hold on the dog to keep him from running through the house. Let the dog have a good shake and dry him with towels.

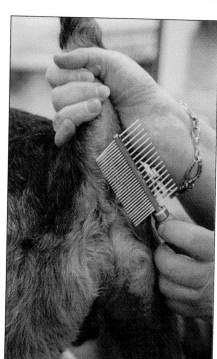

The sensitive tail area should be combed gently with a fine-toothed comb.

EAR CLEANING

The ears should be kept clean and any excess hair inside the ear should be carefully plucked. Ears can be cleaned with a cotton wipe and ear powder made especially for dogs. Be on the lookout for any signs of infection or ear mite infestation. If your Airedale Terrier has been shaking his head or scratching at his ears frequently, this usually indicates a problem. If his ears have an unusual odour, this is a sure sign of mite infestation or infection, and a signal to have his ears checked by the veterinary surgeon.

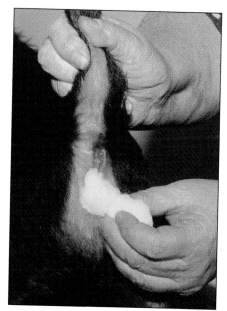

The area around the anal pore should be groomed and cleaned.

NAIL CLIPPING

Your Airedale Terrier should be accustomed to having his nails trimmed at an early age, since it

Nail Maintenance

Nail Casing

Quick

Cut Line

Dark-Coloured Nails

With black or dark nails, where the quick is not easy to see, it's best to clip only the tip of the nail or to use a file.

Light-Coloured Nails

In light-coloured nails, clipping is much simpler because you can see the vein (or quick) that grows inside the casing.

Your dog's nails should be trimmed regularly. When you can hear the nails clicking as the dog walks on a hard surface, the nails are too long. Pet shops sell special clippers for dog's nails.

will be part of your maintenance routine throughout his life. Not only does it look nicer, but long, sharp nails can scratch someone unintentionally. Also, a long nail has a better chance of ripping and bleeding, or causing the feet to spread. A good rule of thumb is that if you can hear your dog's nails clicking on the floor when he walks, his nails are too long.

Before you start cutting, make sure you can identify the 'quick' in each nail. The quick is a blood vessel that runs through the centre of each nail and grows rather close to the end. It will bleed if accidentally cut, which will be quite painful for the dog as it contains nerve endings. Keep some type of clotting agent on hand, such as a styptic pencil or styptic powder (the type used for shaving). This

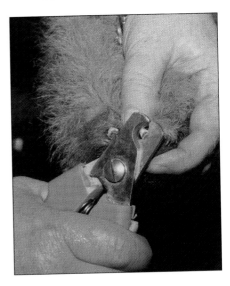

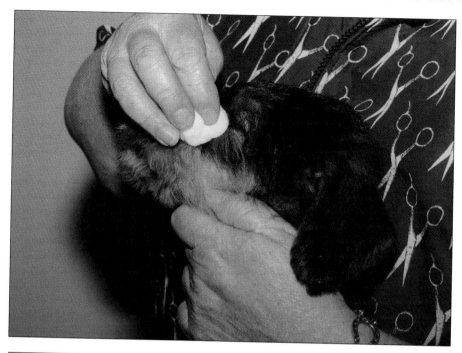

Tear stains under the eye can be removed by using cotton and a special solution available at your pet shop.

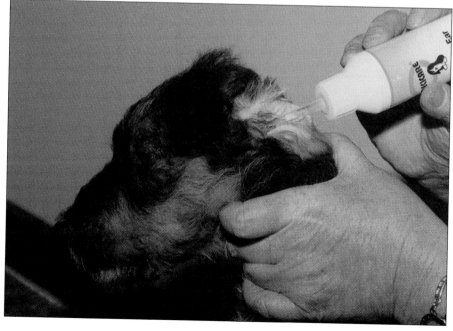

The ears should be attended to using special ear products available from your local pet shop.

clip a little at a time, particularly with black-nailed dogs.

Hold your pup steady as you begin trimming his nails; you do not want him to make any sudden movements or run away. Talk to him soothingly and stroke him as you clip. Holding his foot in your hand, simply take off the end of each nail in one quick clip. You can purchase nail clippers that are specially made for dogs; you can probably find them wherever you buy pet or grooming supplies.

will stop the bleeding quickly when applied to the end of the cut nail. Do not panic if this happens, just stop the bleeding and talk soothingly to your dog. Once he has calmed down, move on to the next nail. It is better to

TRAVELLING WITH YOUR DOG

CAR TRAVEL

You should accustom your Airedale Terrier to riding in a car at an early age. You may or may not take him in the car often, but at the very least he will need to go to the vet and you do not want these trips to be traumatic for the dog or troublesome for you. The safest way for a dog to ride in the car is in his crate. If he uses a crate in the house, you can use the same crate for travel.

Put the pup in the crate and see how he reacts. If he seems uneasy, you can have a passenger hold him on his lap while you drive. Another option is a specially made safety harness for dogs, which straps the dog in much like a seat belt.

Do not let the dog roam loose in the vehicle—this is very dangerous! If you should stop short, your dog can be thrown and injured. If the dog starts climbing on you and pestering you while you are driving, you will not be able to concentrate on the road. It is an unsafe situation for everyone—human and canine.

For long trips, be prepared to stop to let the dog relieve himself. Bring along whatever you need to clean up after him. You should take along some paper kitchen towels and perhaps some old towelling for use should he have an accident in the car or suffer from travel sickness.

AIR TRAVEL

While it is possible to take a dog on a flight within Britain, this is fairly unusual and advance

---

FREE AT LAST!
While running off lead may be great fun for your dog, it can turn into a time when your dog shows you everything you did wrong in obedience class. If you want to give your dog a chance to have some fun and exercise without the constraints of a leash, the best place to do this is in a designated fenced-in area where dogs can socialise and work off excess energy. When visiting such an area, don't let your dog run amok or unattended, watch other dogs that are present, and follow all rules, specifically those regarding waste disposal.

ABUSING YOUR BEST FRIEND
As an educated and caring pet owner, you may believe that everyone wants to invest countless hours (and pounds) in order to raise a loving and well-adjusted canine companion. Sadly, this is not the case, as dogs account for almost half of all victims of animal abuse. Remember, abuse implies not only beating or torturing an animal but also neglecting the animal, such as failing to provide adequate shelter and food or emotional fulfilment.

---

permission is always required. The dog will be required to travel in a fibreglass crate and you should always check in advance with the airline regarding specific requirements. To help the dog be at ease, put one of his favourite toys in the crate with him. Do not feed the dog for at least six hours before the trip to minimise his need to relieve himself. However, certain regulations specify that water must always be made available to the dog in the crate.

Make sure your dog is properly identified and that your contact information appears on his ID tags and on his crate. Animals travel in a different area of the plane than human passen-

Select a well-maintained local boarding kennel before you actually need it. An Airedale is a large dog that needs ample space to exercise properly.

CONSIDERATIONS ABOUT BOARDING

Will your dog be exercised at least twice a day? How much of the day will the staff keep him company? Does the kennel provide a clean and secure environment?

If the staff asks you a lot of questions, this is a good sign. They need to know your dog's personality and temperament, health record, special requirements, and what commands he has learned. Above all, follow your instincts. If you have a bad feeling about one kennel, even if a friend has recommended it, don't put your dog in their care.

gers so every rule must be strictly adhered to so as to prevent the risk of getting separated from your dog.

BOARDING

So you want to take a family holiday—and you want to include all members of the family. You would probably make arrangements for accommodations ahead of time anyway, but this is especially important when travelling with a dog. You do not want to make an overnight stop at the only place around for miles and find out that they do not allow dogs.

Also, you do not want to reserve a place for your family without confirming that you are travelling with a dog because if it is against their policy you may not have a place to stay.

Alternatively, if you are travelling and choose not to bring your Airedale Terrier, you will have to make arrangements for him while you are away. Some options are to take him to a neighbour's house to stay while you are gone, to have a trusted neighbour stop by often or stay at your house, or bring your dog to a reputable boarding kennel. If you choose to board him at a kennel, you should visit in advance to see the facilities provided, how clean they are and where the dogs are kept. Talk to some of the employees and see how they treat the dogs—do they spend time with the dogs, play with them, exercise them, etc.? Also find out the kennel's policy on vaccinations and what they require. This is for all of the dogs' safety, since when dogs are kept together, there is a greater risk of diseases being passed from dog to dog.

IDENTIFICATION
Your Airedale Terrier is your valued companion and friend. That is why you always keep a close eye on him and you have made sure that he cannot escape

IDENTIFICATION
If your dog gets lost, he is not able to ask for directions home.

Identification tags fastened to the collar give important information—the dog's name, the owner's name, the owner's address and a telephone number where the owner can be reached. This makes it easy for whomever finds the dog to contact the owner and arrange to have the dog returned. An added advantage is that a person will be more likely to approach a lost dog who has ID tags on his collar; it tells the person that this is somebody's pet rather than a stray. This is the easiest and fastest method of identification provided that the tags stay on the collar and the collar stays on the dog.

from the garden or wriggle out of his collar and run away from you. However, accidents can happen and there may come a time when your dog unexpectedly gets separated from you. If this unfortunate event should occur, the first thing on your mind will be finding him. Proper identification, including an ID tag, a tattoo and possibly a microchip, will increase the chances of his being returned to you safely and quickly.

Reap the Rewards

If you start with a normal, healthy dog and give him time, patience and some carefully executed lessons, you will reap the rewards of that

training for the life of the dog. And what a life it will be! The two of you will find immeasurable pleasure in the companionship you have built together with love, respect and understanding.

Living with an untrained dog is a lot like owning a piano that you do not know how to play—it is a nice object to look at but it does not do much more than that to bring you pleasure. Now try taking piano lessons and suddenly the piano comes alive and brings forth magical sounds and rhythms that set your heart singing and your body swaying.

The same is true with your Airedale Terrier. Any dog is a big responsibility and if not trained sensibly may develop unacceptable behaviour that annoys you or could even cause family friction.

To train your Airedale Terrier, you may like to enrol in an obedience class. Teach him good manners as you learn how and why he behaves the way he does. Find out how to communicate with your dog and how to recognise and understand his communications with you. Suddenly the dog takes on a new role in your life—he is clever, interesting, well behaved and fun to be with. He demonstrates his bond of devotion to you daily. In other words, your Airedale Terrier does wonders for your ego because he constantly reminds you that you are not only his leader, you are his hero!

Those involved with teaching dog obedience and counselling owners about their dogs' behaviour have discovered some interesting facts about dog ownership. For example, training dogs when they are puppies results in the highest rate of success in developing well-mannered and well-adjusted adult dogs. Training an older dog, from six months to six years of age, can produce almost equal results providing that the owner accepts the dog's slower rate of learning capability and is willing to work patiently to help the dog succeed at developing to his fullest potential. Unfortunately, many owners of untrained adult dogs lack the patience factor, so they do not persist until their dogs are successful at learning particular behaviours.

Training a puppy aged 10 to 16 weeks (20 weeks at the most) is like working with a dry sponge in a pool of water. The pup soaks up whatever you show him and constantly looks for more things to do and learn. At this early age, his body is not yet producing hormones, and therein lies the reason for such a high rate of success. Without hormones, he is focused on his owners and not particularly interested in investigating other

TRAINING TIP
Training a dog is a life experience. Many parents admit that much of what they know about raising children they learned from caring for

their dogs. Dogs respond to love, fairness and guidance, just as children do. Become a good dog owner and you may become an even better parent.

places, dogs, people, etc. You are his leader: his provider of food, water, shelter and security. He latches onto you and wants to stay close. He will usually

because that would be his normal response. This is not aggressive biting and, although all biting should be discouraged, you need the discipline in learning how to handle your dog.

follow you from room to room, will not let you out of his sight when you are outdoors with him, and respond in like manner to the people and animals you encounter. If you greet a friend warmly, he will be happy to greet the person as well. If, however, you are hesitant, even anxious, about the approach of a stranger, he will respond accordingly.

Once the puppy begins to produce hormones, his natural curiosity emerges and he begins to investigate the world around him. It is at this time when you may notice that the untrained dog begins to wander away from you and even ignore your commands to stay close. When this behaviour becomes a problem, the owner has two choices: get rid of the dog or train him. It is strongly urged that you choose the latter option.

There are usually classes within a reasonable distance from the owner's home, but you also do a lot to train your dog yourself. Sometimes there are classes available but the tuition is too costly. Whatever the circumstances, the solution to the problem of lack of lesson availability lies within the pages of this book.

This chapter is devoted to helping you train your Airedale Terrier at home. If the recommended procedures are followed faithfully, you may expect positive results that will prove rewarding to both you and your dog.

Whether your new charge is

Housebreaking and Training

a puppy or a mature adult, the methods of teaching and the techniques we use in training basic behaviours are the same. After all, no dog, whether puppy or adult, likes harsh or inhumane methods. All creatures, however, respond favourably to gentle motivational methods and sincere praise and encouragement. Now let us get started.

HOUSEBREAKING

You can train a puppy to relieve itself wherever you choose, but this must be somewhere suitable. You should bear in mind from the outset that when your puppy is old enough to go out in public places, any canine deposits must be removed at once. You will always have to carry with you a small plastic bag or 'poop-scoop.'

Outdoor training includes

MEALTIME
Mealtime should be a peaceful time for your puppy. Do not put his food and water bowls in a high-traffic area in the house. For example, give him his own little corner of the kitchen where he can eat undisturbed and where he will not be under foot. Do not allow small children or other family members to disturb the pup when he is eating.

Think Before You Bark!

Dogs are sensitive to their master's moods and emotions. Use your voice wisely when communicating with your dog. Never raise your voice at your dog unless you are angry and trying to correct him. 'Barking' at your dog can become as meaningless as 'dogspeak' is to you. Think before you bark!

such surfaces as grass, mud, soil or earth and cement. Indoor training usually means training your dog to newspaper.

When deciding on the surface and location that you will want your Airedale Terrier to use, be sure it is going to be permanent. Training your dog to grass and then changing your mind two months later is extremely difficult for both dog and owner.

Next, choose the command

Training Tip

Dogs will do anything for your attention. If you reward the dog when he is calm and resting, you will develop a well-mannered dog. If, on the

other hand, you greet your dog excitedly and encourage him to wrestle with you, the dog will greet you the same way and you will have a hyperactive dog on your hands.

you will use each and every time you want your puppy to void. 'Be quick' and 'Hurry up' are examples of commands commonly used by dog owners.

Get in the habit of giving the puppy your chosen relief command before you take him out. That way, when he becomes an adult, you will be able to determine if he wants to go out when you ask him. A confirmation will be signs of interest, wagging his tail, watching you intently, going to the door, etc.

PUPPY'S NEEDS

Puppy needs to relieve himself after play periods, after each meal, after he has been sleeping and any time he indicates that he is looking for a place to urinate or defecate.

The urinary and intestinal tract muscles of very young puppies are not fully developed. Therefore, like human babies, puppies need to relieve themselves frequently.

Take your puppy out often— every hour for an eight-week-old, for example, and always immediately after sleeping and eating. The older the puppy, the less often he will need to relieve himself. Finally, as a mature healthy adult, he will require only three to five relief trips per day.

HOUSING

Since the types of housing and control you provide for your puppy has a direct relationship on the success of housetraining, we consider the various aspects of both before we begin training.

Bringing a new puppy home and turning him loose in your house can be compared to turning a child loose in a sports arena and telling the child that the place is all his! The sheer enormity of the place would be too much for him to handle.

Instead, offer the puppy clearly defined areas where he

CANINE DEVELOPMENT SCHEDULE

It is important to understand how and at what age a puppy develops into adulthood. If you are a puppy owner, consult the following Canine Development Schedule to determine the stage of development your puppy is currently experiencing. This knowledge will help you as you work with the puppy in the weeks and months ahead.

Period	Age	Characteristics
FIRST TO THIRD	**BIRTH TO SEVEN WEEKS**	Puppy needs food, sleep and warmth, and responds to simple and gentle touching. Needs mother for security and disciplining. Needs littermates for learning and interacting with other dogs. Pup learns to function within a pack and learns pack order of dominance. Begin socialising with adults and children for short periods. Begins to become aware of its environment.
FOURTH	**EIGHT TO TWELVE WEEKS**	Brain is fully developed. Needs socialising with outside world. Remove from mother and littermates. Needs to change from canine pack to human pack. Human dominance necessary. Fear period occurs between 8 and 16 weeks. Avoid fright and pain.
FIFTH	**THIRTEEN TO SIXTEEN WEEKS**	Training and formal obedience should begin. Less association with other dogs, more with people, places, situations. Period will pass easily if you remember this is pup's change-to-adolescence time. Be firm and fair. Flight instinct prominent. Permissiveness and over-disciplining can do permanent damage. Praise for good behaviour.
JUVENILE	**FOUR TO EIGHT MONTHS**	Another fear period about 7 to 8 months of age. It passes quickly, but be cautious of fright and pain. Sexual maturity reached. Dominant traits established. Dog should understand sit, down, come and stay by now.

NOTE: THESE ARE APPROXIMATE TIME FRAMES. ALLOW FOR INDIVIDUAL DIFFERENCES IN PUPPIES.

DID YOU KNOW?
Never line your pup's sleeping area with newspaper. Puppy litters are usually raised on newspaper and, once in your home, the puppy will immediately associate newspaper with voiding. Never put newspaper on any floor while housetraining, as this

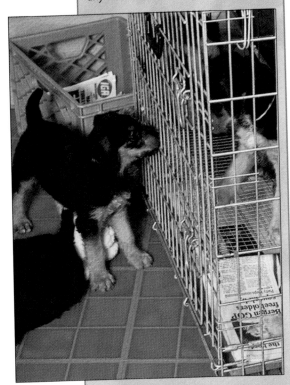

will only confuse the puppy. If you are paper-training him, use paper in his designated relief area ONLY. Finally, restrict water intake after evening meals. Offer a few licks at a time—never let a young puppy gulp water after meals.

can play, sleep, eat and live. A room of the house where the family gathers is the most obvious choice. Puppies are social animals and need to feel a part of the pack right from the start. Hearing your voice, watching you while you are doing things and smelling you nearby are all positive reinforcers that he is now a member of your pack. Usually a family room, the kitchen or a nearby adjoining breakfast area is ideal for providing safety and security for both puppy and owner.

Within that room there should be a smaller area which the puppy can call his own. An alcove, a wire or fibreglass dog crate or a fenced (not boarded!) corner from which he can view the activities of his new family will be fine. The size of the area or crate is the key factor here. The area must be large enough for the puppy to lie down and

DID YOU KNOW?
Dogs are the most honourable animals in existence. They consider another species (humans) as their own. They interface with you. You are their leader. Puppies perceive children to be on their level; their actions around small children are different from their behaviour around their adult masters.

CONTROL

By control, we mean helping the puppy to create a lifestyle pattern that will be compatible to that of his human pack (YOU!). Just as we guide little children to learn our way of life, we must show the puppy when it is time to play, eat, sleep, exercise and even entertain himself.

Your puppy should always sleep in his crate. He should also learn that, during times of household confusion and excessive human activity such as at breakfast when family members are preparing for the day, he can play by himself in relative safety and comfort in his designated area. Each time you leave the puppy alone, he should understand exactly where he is to stay. Puppies are chewers. They cannot tell the difference between lamp cords, television wires, shoes, table legs, etc. Chewing into a television wire, for example, can be fatal to the puppy while a

Experienced breeders introduce their Airedale puppies to crates at a young age. Such puppies will welcome a crate when they arrive at their new homes.

stretch out as well as stand up without rubbing his head on the top, yet small enough so that he cannot relieve himself at one end and sleep at the other without coming into contact with his droppings until fully trained to relieve himself outside.

Dogs are, by nature, clean animals and will not remain close to their relief areas unless forced to do so. In those cases, they then become dirty dogs and usually remain that way for life.

The designated area should be lined with clean bedding and contain a toy. Water must always be available, in a non-spill container.

When buying a crate for your Airedale, get the largest size available to accommodate your dog.

Airedale Terrier

Lead your Airedale puppy to the same place to relieve himself every time. He will quickly learn the routine and will always return to 'his' spot.

DID YOU KNOW?
Do not carry your dog to his toilet area. Lead him there on a leash or, better yet, encourage him to follow you to the spot. If you start carrying him to his spot, you might end up doing this routine forever and your dog will have the satisfaction of having trained YOU.

shorted wire can start a fire in the house.

If the puppy chews on the arm of the chair when he is alone, you will probably discipline him angrily when you get home. Thus, he makes the association that your coming home means he is going to be punished. (He will not remember chewing up the chair and is incapable of making the association of the discipline with his naughty deed.)

Other times of excitement, such as family parties, etc., can be fun for the puppy providing he can view the activities from the security of his designated area. He is not underfoot and he is not being fed all sorts of titbits that will probably cause him stomach distress, yet he still feels a part of the fun.

SCHEDULE

A puppy should be taken to his relief area each time he is released from his designated area, after meals, after a play session, when he first awakens in the morning (at age eight weeks, this can mean 5 a.m.!). The puppy will indicate that he's ready 'to go' by circling or sniffing busily—do not misinterpret these signs. For a puppy less than ten weeks of age, a routine of taking him out every hour is necessary. As the puppy grows, he will be able to wait for

THE GOLDEN RULE
The golden rule of dog training is simple. For each 'question' (command), there is only one correct answer (reaction). One command = one reaction. Keep practising the command until the dog reacts correctly without hesitating. Be repetitive but not monotonous. Dogs get bored just as people do!

longer periods of time.

Keep trips to his relief area short. Stay no more than five or six minutes and then return to the house. If he goes during that time, praise him lavishly and take him indoors immediately. If he does not, but he has an accident when you go back indoors, pick him up immediately, say 'No! No!' and return to his relief area. Wait a few minutes, then return to the house again. Never hit a puppy or rub his face in urine or excrement when he has an accident!

Once indoors, put the puppy in his crate until you have had time to clean up his accident. Then release him to the family area and watch him more closely than before. Chances are, his accident was a result of your not picking up his signal or waiting too long before offering him the opportunity to relieve himself.

HOW MANY TIMES A DAY?

AGE	RELIEF TRIPS
To 14 weeks	10
14–22 weeks	8
22–32 weeks	6
Adulthood	4
(dog stops growing)	

These are estimates, of course, but they are a guide to the MINIMUM opportunities a dog should have each day to relieve itself.

PRACTICE MAKES PERFECT!

• Have training lessons with your dog every day in several short segments— three to five times a day for a few minutes at a time is ideal.
• Do not have long practice sessions. The dog will become easily bored.
• Never practise when you are tired, ill, worried or in an otherwise negative mood. This will transmit to the dog and may have an adverse effect on its performance.

Think fun, short and above all POSITIVE! End each session on a high note, rather than a failed exercise, and make sure to give a lot of praise. Enjoy the training and help your dog enjoy it, too.

Housebreaking Tip

Most of all, be consistent. Always take your dog to the same location, always use the same command, and always have him on lead when he is in his relief area, unless a fenced-in garden is available.

By following the Success Method, your puppy will be completely housetrained by the time his muscle and brain development reach maturity. Keep in mind that small breeds usually mature faster than large breeds, but all puppies should be trained by six months of age.

playing by himself and just resting, all in his crate. Encourage him to entertain himself while you are busy with your activities. Let him learn that having you near is comforting, but it is not your main purpose in life to provide him with undivided attention.

Each time you put a puppy in his own area, use the same command, whatever suits best. Soon, he will run to his crate or special area when he hears you say those words.

Crate training provides safety for you, the puppy and the home. It also provides the puppy with a feeling of security, and that helps the puppy achieve self-confidence and clean habits.

Remember that one of the primary ingredients in housetraining your puppy is control. Regardless of your lifestyle, there will always be occasions when you will need to

Never hold a grudge against the puppy for accidents.

Let the puppy learn that going outdoors means it is time to relieve himself, not play. Once trained, he will be able to play indoors and out and still differentiate between the times for play versus the times for relief.

Help him develop regular hours for naps, being alone,

THE SUCCESS METHOD

Success that comes by luck is usually short lived. Success that comes by well-thought-out proven methods is often more easily achieved and permanent. This is the Success Method. It is designed to give you, the puppy owner, a simple yet proven way to help your puppy develop clean living habits and a feeling of security in his new environment.

DID YOU KNOW?

By providing sleeping and resting quarters that fit the dog, and offering frequent opportunities to relieve himself outside his quarters, the puppy quickly learns that the outdoors (or the newspaper if you are training him to paper) is the place to go when he needs to urinate or defecate. It also reinforces his innate desire to keep his sleeping quarters clean. This, in turn, helps develop the muscle control that will eventually produce a dog with clean living habits.

have a place where your dog can stay and be happy and safe. Training is the answer for now and in the future.

In conclusion, a few key elements are really all you need for a successful house training method—consistency, frequency, praise, control and supervision. By following these procedures with a normal, healthy puppy, you and the puppy will soon be past the stage of 'accidents' and ready to move on to a full and rewarding life together.

THE SUCCESS METHOD

1 Tell the puppy 'Crate time!' and place him in the crate with a small treat (a piece of cheese or half of a biscuit). Let him stay in the crate for five minutes while you are in the same room. Then release him and praise lavishly. Never release him when he is fussing. Wait until he is quiet before you let him out.

2 Repeat Step 1 several times a day.

3 The next day, place the puppy in the crate as before. Let him stay there for ten minutes. Do this several times.

4 Continue building time in five-minute increments until the puppy stays in his crate for 30 minutes with you in the room. Always take him to his relief area after prolonged periods in his crate.

5 Now go back to Step 1 and let the puppy stay in his crate for five minutes, this time while you are out of the room.

6 Once again, build crate time in five-minute increments with you out of the room. When the puppy will stay willingly in his crate (he may even fall asleep!) for 30 minutes with you out of the room, he will be ready to stay in it for several hours at a time.

6 Steps to Successful Crate Training

TRAINING TIP

Stand up straight and authoritatively when giving your dog commands. Do

not issue commands when lying on the floor or lying on your back on the sofa. If you are on your hands and knees when you give a command, your dog will think you are positioning yourself to play.

ROLES OF DISCIPLINE, REWARD AND PUNISHMENT

Discipline, training one to act in accordance with rules, brings order to life. It is as simple as that. Without discipline, particularly in a group society, chaos reigns supreme and the group will eventually perish. Humans and canines are social animals and need some form of discipline in order to function effectively. They must procure food, protect their home base and their young and reproduce to keep the species going.

If there were no discipline in the lives of social animals, they would eventually die from starvation and/or predation by other stronger animals.

In the case of domestic canines, dogs need discipline in their lives in order to understand how their pack (you and other family members) functions and how they must act in order to survive.

A large humane society in a highly populated area recently surveyed dog owners regarding their satisfaction with their relationships with their dogs.

DID YOU KNOW?

Dogs are as different from each other as people are. What works for one dog may not work for another. Have an open mind. If one method of training is unsuccessful, try another.

People who had trained their dogs were 75% more satisfied with their pets than those who had never trained their dogs.

Dr Edward Thorndike, a psychologist, established *Thorndike's Theory of Learning*, which states that a behaviour that results in a pleasant event tends to be repeated. A behaviour that results in an unpleasant event tends not to be repeated. It is this theory on which training methods are based today. For example, if you manipulate a dog to perform a specific behaviour and reward him for doing it, he is likely to do it again because he enjoyed the end result.

Occasionally, punishment, a penalty inflicted for an offence, is necessary. The best type of punishment often comes from an outside source. For example, a child is told

TRAINING RULES

If you want to be successful in training your dog, you have four rules to obey yourself:
1. Develop an understanding of how a dog thinks.
2. Do not blame the dog for lack of communication.
3. Define your dog's personality and act accordingly.
4. Have patience and be consistent.

Training Tip

Dogs do not understand our language. They can be trained to react to a certain sound, at a certain volume. If you say 'No, Oliver' in a very soft pleasant voice it will not have the same meaning as 'No, Oliver!!' when you shout it as loud as you can. You should never use the dog's name during a reprimand, just the command NO!! Since dogs don't understand words, comics often use dogs trained with opposite meanings. Thus, when the comic commands his dog to SIT the dog will stand up, and vice versa.

not to touch the stove because he may get burned. He disobeys and touches the stove. In doing so, he receives a burn. From that time on, he respects the heat of the stove and avoids contact with it. Therefore, a behaviour that results in an unpleasant event tends not to be repeated.

A good example of a dog learning the hard way is the dog who chases the house cat. He is told many times to leave the cat alone, yet he persists in teasing the cat. Then, one day he begins chasing the cat but the cat turns and swipes a claw across the dog's face, leaving him with a painful gash on his nose. The final result is that the dog stops chasing the cat.

TRAINING EQUIPMENT

COLLAR AND LEAD
For an Airedale Terrier the collar and lead that you use for training must be one with which you are easily able to work, not too heavy for the dog and perfectly safe.

TREATS
Have a bag of treats on hand. Something nutritious and easy to swallow works best. Use a soft treat, a chunk of cheese or a piece of cooked chicken rather than a dry biscuit. By the time the dog has finished chewing a dry treat, he will forget why he

is being rewarded in the first place! Using food rewards will not teach a dog to beg at the table—the only way to teach a dog to beg at the table is to give him food from the table. In training, rewarding the dog with a food treat will help him associate praise and the treats with learning new behaviours that obviously please his owner.

TRAINING BEGINS: ASK THE DOG A QUESTION
In order to teach your dog anything, you must first get his attention. After all, he cannot learn anything if he is looking away from you with his mind on something else.

To get his attention, ask him, 'School?' and immediately walk over to him and give him a treat as you tell him 'Good dog.' Wait a minute or two and repeat the routine, this time with a treat in your hand as you approach within a foot of the dog. Do not go directly to him, but stop about a foot short of him and hold out the treat as you ask, 'School?' He will see you approaching with a treat in your

Opposite page: The training collar and lead should be light for the puppy. As the dog grows so should the sturdiness of the collar and lead. Use treats wisely when training your puppy.

Training Tip

Never train your dog, puppy or adult, when you are angry or in a sour mood. Dogs are very sensitive to human feelings, especially

anger, and if your dog senses that you are angry or upset, he will connect your anger with his training and learn to resent or fear his training sessions.

him the treat and praise again.

By this time, the dog will probably be getting the idea that if he pays attention to you, especially when you ask that question, it will pay off in treats and fun activities for him. In other words, he learns that 'school' means doing fun things with you that result in treats and positive attention for him.

Remember that the dog does not understand your verbal language, he only recognises sounds. Your question translates to a series of sounds for him, and those sounds become the signal to go to you and pay attention; if he does, he will get to interact with you plus receive treats and praise.

THE BASIC COMMANDS

TEACHING SIT

Now that you have the dog's attention, attach his lead and hold it in your left hand and a food treat in your right. Place your food hand at the dog's nose and let him lick the treat but not take it from you. Say 'Sit' and slowly raise your food hand from in front of the dog's nose up over his head so that he is looking at the ceiling. As he bends his head upward, he will have to bend his knees to maintain his balance. As he bends his knees, he will assume a sit position. At that point,

hand and most likely begin walking toward you. As you meet, give him the treat and praise again.

The third time, ask the question, have a treat in your hand and walk only a short distance toward the dog so that he must walk almost all the way to you. As he reaches you, give

FEAR AGGRESSION

Pups who are subjected to physical abuse during training commonly end up with behavioural problems as adults. One common result of abuse is fear aggression, in which a dog will lash out, bare his teeth, snarl and finally bite someone by whom he feels threatened. For example, your daughter may be playing with the dog one afternoon. As they play hide-and-seek, she backs the dog into a corner, and as she attempts to tease him playfully, he bites her hand. Examine the cause of this behaviour. Did your daughter ever hit the dog? Did someone who resembles your daughter hit or scream at the dog? Fortunately, fear aggression is relatively easy to correct. Have your daughter engage in only positive activities with the dog, such as feeding, petting and walking. She should not give any corrections or negative feedback. If the dog still growls or cowers away from her, allow someone else to accompany them. After approximately one week, the dog should feel that he can rely on her for many positive things, and he will also be prevented from reacting fearfully towards anyone who might resemble her.

Training must be treated in a serious manner. Many puppies cannot focus on the lesson at hand. Be patient, consistent and fair. 'Sit' is the starting point of most trainers.

relish verbal praise from their owners and feel so proud of themselves whenever they accomplish a behaviour.

You will not use food forever in getting the dog to obey your commands. Food is only used to teach new behaviours, and once the dog knows what you want when you give a specific command, you will wean him off of the food treats but still maintain the verbal praise. After all, you will always have your voice with you, and there will be many times when you have no food rewards but expect the dog to obey.

release the food treat and praise lavishly with comments such as 'Good dog! Good sit!', etc. Remember to always praise enthusiastically, because dogs

Training Tip

A dog in jeopardy never lies down. He stays alert on his feet because instinct tells him that he may have to run away or fight for his

survival. Therefore, if a dog feels threatened or anxious, he will not lie down. Consequently, it is important to have the dog calm and relaxed as he learns the down exercise.

TEACHING DOWN

Teaching the down exercise is easy when you understand how the dog perceives the down position, and it is very difficult when you do not. Dogs perceive the down position as a submissive one, therefore teaching the down exercise using a forceful method can sometimes make the dog develop such a fear of the down that he either runs away when you say 'Down' or he attempts to snap at the person who tries to force him down.

Have the dog sit close alongside your left leg, facing in the same direction as you are. Hold the lead in your left hand and a food treat in your right. Now place your left hand lightly on the top of the dog's shoulders where they meet above the spinal cord. Do not push down on the dog's shoulders; simply rest your left hand there so you can guide the dog to lie down close to your left leg rather than to swing away from your side when he drops.

Now place the food hand at the dog's nose, say 'Down' very softly (almost a whisper), and slowly lower the food hand to the dog's front feet. When the food hand reaches the floor, begin moving it forward along the floor in front of the dog. Keep talking softly to the dog, saying things like, 'Do you want this treat? You can do this, good dog.' Your reassuring tone of voice will help calm the dog as he tries to follow the food hand in order to get the treat.

When the dog's elbows touch the floor, release the food and praise softly. Try to get the dog to maintain that down position for several seconds before you let him sit up again. The goal here is to get the dog to settle down and not feel threatened in the down position.

TEACHING STAY

It is easy to teach the dog to stay in either a sit or a down position. Again, we use food and praise during the teaching process as we help the dog to understand exactly what it is that we are expecting him to do.

To teach the sit/stay, start with the dog sitting on your left side as before and hold the lead in your left hand. Have a food treat in your right hand and place your food hand at the dog's nose. Say 'Stay' and step out on your right foot to stand directly in front of the dog, toe to toe, as he licks and nibbles the treat. Be sure to keep his head facing upward to maintain the sit position. Count to five and then swing around to stand next to the dog again with him on your left. As soon as you get back to the original position, release the food and praise lavishly.

To teach the down/stay, do the down as previously described. As soon as the dog lies down, say 'Stay' and step out on your right foot just as you did in the sit/stay. Count to five and then return to stand beside the dog with him on your left side. Release the treat and praise as always.

Within a week or ten days, you can begin to add a bit of distance between you and your dog when you leave him. When

THE STUDENT'S STRESS TEST

During training sessions you must be able to recognise signs of stress in your dog such as:
- tucking his tail between his legs
- lowering his head
- shivering or trembling
- standing completely still or running away
- panting and/or salivating
- avoiding eye contact
- flattening his ears back

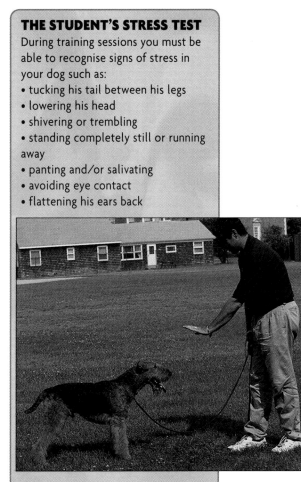

- urinating submissively
- rolling over and lifting a leg
- grinning or baring teeth
- aggression when restrained

If your four-legged student displays these signs he may just be nervous or intimidated. The training session may have been too lengthy with not enough praise and affirmation. Stop for the day and try again tomorrow.

SAFETY FIRST

While it may seem that the most important things to your dog are eating, sleeping and chewing the upholstery on your furniture, his first concern is actually safety. The domesticated dogs we keep as companions have the same pack instinct as their ancestors who ran free thousands of years ago. Because of this pack instinct, your dog wants to know that he and his pack are not in danger of being harmed, and that his pack has a strong, capable leader. You must establish yourself as the leader early on in your relationship. That way your dog will trust that you will take care of him and the pack, and he will accept your commands without question.

stay position for prolonged periods of time until you return to him or call him to you. Always praise lavishly when he stays.

TEACHING COME

If you make teaching 'come' a fun experience, you should never have a 'student' that does not love the game or that fails to come when called. The secret, it seems, is never to teach the word 'come.'

At times when an owner most wants his dog to come when called, the owner is likely upset or anxious and he allows these feelings to come through in the tone of his voice when he calls his dog. Hearing that desperation in his owner's voice, the dog fears the results of going to him and therefore either

you do, use your left hand open with the palm facing the dog as a stay signal, much the same as the hand signal a police officer uses to stop traffic at an intersection. Hold the food treat in your right hand as before, but this time the food is not touching the dog's nose. He will watch the food hand and quickly learn that he is going to get that treat as soon as you return to his side.

When you can stand 1 metre away from your dog for 30 seconds, you can then begin building time and distance in both stays. Eventually, the dog can be expected to remain in the

CONSISTENCY PAYS OFF

Dogs need consistency in their feeding schedule, exercise and toilet breaks and in the verbal commands you use. If you use 'Stay' on Monday and 'Stay here, please' on Tuesday, you will confuse your dog. Don't demand perfect behaviour during training classes and then let him have the run of the house the rest of the day. Above all, lavish praise on your pet consistently every time he does something right. The more he feels he is pleasing you, the more willing he will be to learn.

disobeys outright or runs in the opposite direction. The secret, therefore, is to teach the dog a game and, when you want him to come to you, simply play the game. It is practically a no-fail solution!

To begin, have several members of your family take a few food treats and each go into a different room in the house. Take turns calling the dog, and each person should celebrate the dog's finding him with a treat and lots of happy praise. When a person calls the dog, he is actually inviting the dog to find him and get a treat as a reward for 'winning.'

A few turns of the 'Where are you?' game and the dog will understand that everyone is playing the game and that each person has a big celebration awaiting his success at locating them. Once he learns to love the game, simply calling out 'Where are you?' will bring him running from wherever he is when he

TRAINING TIP

When calling the dog, do not say 'Come.' Say things like, 'Rover, where are you? See if you can find me! I have a biscuit for you!' Keep up a constant line of chatter with coaxing sounds and frequent questions such as, 'Where are you?' The dog will learn to follow the sound of your voice to locate you and receive his reward.

hears that all-important question.

The come command is recognised as one of the most important things to teach a dog, but there are trainers who work with thousands of dogs and never teach the actual word 'Come.' Yet these dogs will race to respond to a person who uses the dog's name followed by 'Where are you?' For example, a woman has a 12-year-old companion dog who went blind, but who never fails to locate her owner when asked, 'Where are you?'

Children particularly love to play this game with their dogs. Children can hide in smaller places like a shower or bath, behind a bed or under a table. The dog needs to work a little bit harder to find these hiding places, but when he does he loves to celebrate with a treat and a tussle with a favourite youngster.

TRAINING TIP

Never call your dog to come to you for a correction or scold him when he reaches you. That is the quickest way to turn a 'Come' command into 'Go away fast!' Dogs think only in the present tense, and your dog will connect the scolding with coming to you, not with the misbehaviour of a few moments earlier.

TEACHING HEEL

Heeling means that the dog walks beside the owner without pulling. It takes time and patience on the owner's part to succeed at teaching the dog that he (the owner) will not proceed unless the dog is walking calmly beside him. Pulling out ahead on the lead is definitely not acceptable.

Begin with holding the lead in your left hand as the dog sits beside your left leg. Move the loop end of the lead to your right hand but keep your left hand short on the lead so it keeps the dog in close next to you.

Say 'Heel' and step forward on your left foot. Keep the dog close to you and take three steps. Stop and have the dog sit next to you in what we now call the 'heel position.' Praise verbally, but do not touch the dog. Hesitate a moment and begin again with 'Heel,' taking three steps and stopping, at which point the dog is told to sit again.

Your goal here is to have the dog walk those three steps without pulling on the lead. When he will walk calmly beside you for three steps without pulling, increase the number of steps you take to five. When he will walk politely beside you while you take five steps, you can increase the length of your walk to ten steps. Keep increasing the length of your stroll until the dog will walk quietly beside you without pulling as long as you want him to heel. When you stop heeling, indicate to the dog that the exercise is over by verbally praising as you pet him and say 'OK, good dog.' The 'OK' is used as a release word meaning that the exercise is finished and the dog is free to relax.

If you are dealing with a dog

who insists on pulling you around, simply 'put on your brakes' and stand your ground until the dog realises that the two of you are not going anywhere until he is beside you and moving at your pace, not his. It may take some time just standing there to convince the dog that you are the leader and you will be the one to decide on the direction and speed of your travel.

Each time the dog looks up at you or slows down to give a slack lead between the two of you, quietly praise him and say, 'Good heel. Good dog.' Eventually, the dog will begin to respond and within a few days he will be walking politely beside you without pulling on the lead. At first, the training sessions should be kept short and very positive; soon the dog will be able to walk nicely with you for increasingly longer distances. Remember also to give the dog free time and the opportunity to run and play when you have finished heel practice.

TRAINING TIP
If you are walking your dog and he suddenly stops and looks straight into your eyes, ignore him. Pull the leash and lead him into the direction you want to walk.

Training Tip

If you begin teaching the heel by taking long walks and letting the dog pull you along, he misinterprets this action as an acceptable form of taking a walk. When you pull back on the lead to counteract his pulling, he reads that tug as a signal to pull even harder!

Show dogs must master the heel lesson in order to gait properly in the show ring.

WEANING OFF FOOD IN TRAINING

Food is used in training new behaviours. Once the dog understands what behaviour goes with a specific command, it is time to start weaning him off the food treats. At first, give a treat after each exercise. Then, start to give a treat only after every other exercise. Mix up the times when you offer a food reward and the times when you only offer praise so that the dog will never know when he is going to receive both food and praise and when he is going to receive only praise. This is called a variable ratio reward system and it proves successful

because there is always the chance that the owner will produce a treat, so the dog never stops trying for that reward. No matter what, ALWAYS give verbal praise.

OBEDIENCE CLASSES

It is a good idea to enrol in an obedience class if one is available in your area. If yours is a show dog, ringcraft classes would be more appropriate. Many areas have dog clubs that offer basic obedience training as well as preparatory classes for obedience competition. There are also local dog trainers who offer similar classes.

At obedience trials, dogs can earn titles at various levels of competition. The beginning levels of competition include basic behaviours such as sit, down, heel, etc. The more advanced levels of competition include jumping, retrieving, scent discrimination and signal work. The advanced levels require a dog and owner to put a lot of time and effort into their

TRAINING TIP
Teach your dog to HEEL in an enclosed area. Once you think the dog will obey reliably and you want to attempt advanced obedience exercises such as off-lead heeling, test him in a fenced-in area so he cannot run away.

training and the titles that can be earned at these levels of competition are very prestigious.

OTHER ACTIVITIES FOR LIFE
Whether a dog is trained in the structured environment of a class or alone with his owner at home, there are many activities that can bring fun and rewards to both owner and dog once they have mastered basic control.

Teaching the dog to help out around the home, in the garden or on the farm provides great satisfaction to both dog and owner. In addition, the dog's help makes life a little easier for his owner and raises his stature as a valued companion to his family. It helps give the dog a purpose by occupying his mind and providing an outlet for his energy.

Backpacking is an exciting and healthy activity that the dog can be taught without assistance from more than his owner. The exercise of walking and climbing is good for man and dog alike, and the bond that they develop together is priceless.

If you are interested in participating in organised competition with your Airedale Terrier, there are activities other than obedience in which you and your dog can become involved. Agility is a popular and fun sport where dogs run through an obstacle course that includes various jumps, tunnels and other exercises to test the dog's speed and coordination. The owners run through the course beside their dogs to give commands and to guide them through the course. Although competitive, the focus is on fun—it's fun to do, fun to watch, and great exercise.

TRAINING TIP
Your dog is actually training you at the same time you are training him.

Dogs do things to get attention. They usually repeat whatever succeeds in getting your attention.

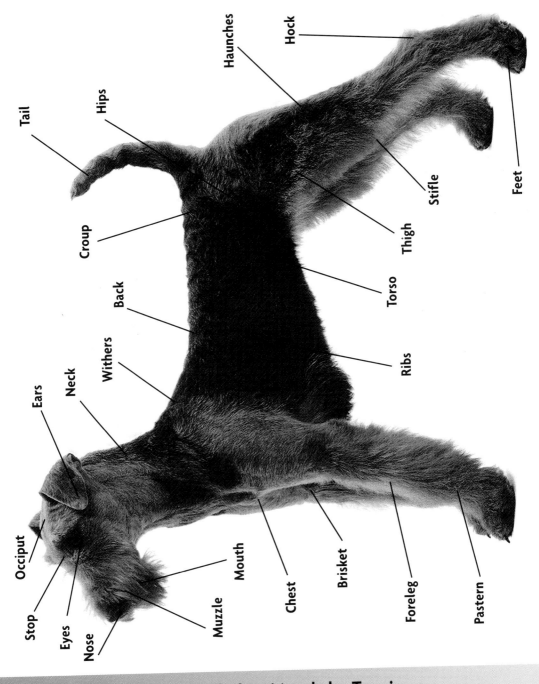

Physical Structure of the Airedale Terrier

Haunches

Hock

Tail

Hips

Stifle

Feet

Croup

Thigh

Back

Torso

Withers

Neck

Ribs

Ears

Occiput

Stop

Eyes

Nose

Muzzle

Mouth

Chest

Brisket

Foreleg

Pastern

Dogs suffer many of the same physical illnesses as people. They might even share many of the same psychological problems. Since people usually know more about human diseases than canine maladies, many of the terms used in this chapter will be familiar but not necessarily those used by veterinary surgeons. We will use the term *x-ray*, instead of the more acceptable term *radiograph*. We will also use the familiar term *symptoms* even though dogs don't have symptoms, which are verbal descriptions of the patient's feelings: dogs have *clinical signs*. Since dogs can't speak, we have to look for clinical signs...but we still use the term symptoms in this book.

As a general rule, medicine is practised. That term is not arbitrary. Medicine is a constantly changing art as we learn more and more about genetics, electronic

aids (like CAT scans) and daily laboratory advances. There are many dog maladies, like canine hip dysplasia, which are not universally treated in the same manner. Some veterinary surgeons opt for surgery more often than others do.

SELECTING A VETERINARY SURGEON

Your selection of a veterinary surgeon should not be based upon personality (as most are) but upon their convenience to your home. You require a veterinary surgeon who is close because you might have emergencies or need to make multiple visits for treatments. You require a vet who has services that you might require such as a tattooing and grooming facilities, as well as sophisticated pet supplies and a good reputation for ability and responsiveness. There

Before you buy a dog, meet and interview the veterinary surgeons in your area. Take everything into consideration; discuss background, specialities, fees, emergency policies, etc.

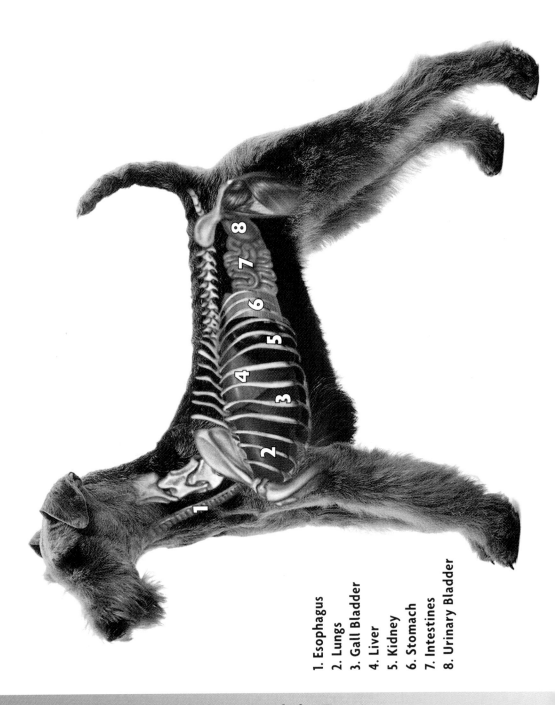

1. Esophagus
2. Lungs
3. Gall Bladder
4. Liver
5. Kidney
6. Stomach
7. Intestines
8. Urinary Bladder

Internal Organs of the Airedale Terrier

is nothing more frustrating than having to wait a day or more to get a response from your veterinary surgeon.

All veterinary surgeons are licensed and their diplomas and/or certificates should be displayed in their waiting rooms. There are, however, many veterinary specialities that usually require further studies and internships. There are specialists in heart problems (veterinary cardiologists), skin problems (veterinary dermatologists), teeth and gum problems (veterinary dentists), eye problems (veterinary ophthalmologists) and x-rays (veterinary radiologists), and surgeons who have specialities in bones, muscles or other organs. Most veterinary surgeons do routine surgery such as neutering, stitching up wounds and docking tails for those breeds in which such is required for show purposes. When the problem affecting your dog is serious, it is not unusual or impudent to get another medical opinion,

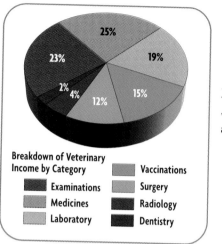

Breakdown of Veterinary Income by Category

	Vaccinations
Examinations	Surgery
Medicines	Radiology
Laboratory	Dentistry

A typical American vet's income, categorised according to services provided. This survey dealt with small-animal practices.

although in Britain you are obliged to advise the vets concerned about this. You might also want to compare costs among several veterinary surgeons. Sophisticated health care and veterinary services can be very costly. Don't be bashful about discussing these costs with your veterinary surgeon or his (her) staff. It is not infrequent that important decisions are based upon financial considerations.

PREVENTATIVE MEDICINE
It is much easier, less costly and more effective to practise preventative medicine than to fight bouts of illness and disease. Properly bred puppies come from parents that were selected based upon their genetic disease profile. Their mothers should have been vaccinated, free of all internal and external parasites and properly

DID YOU KNOW?
Male dogs are neutered. The operation removes the testicles and requires that the dog be anaesthetised. Recovery takes about one week. Females are spayed. This is major surgery and it usually takes a bitch two weeks to recover.

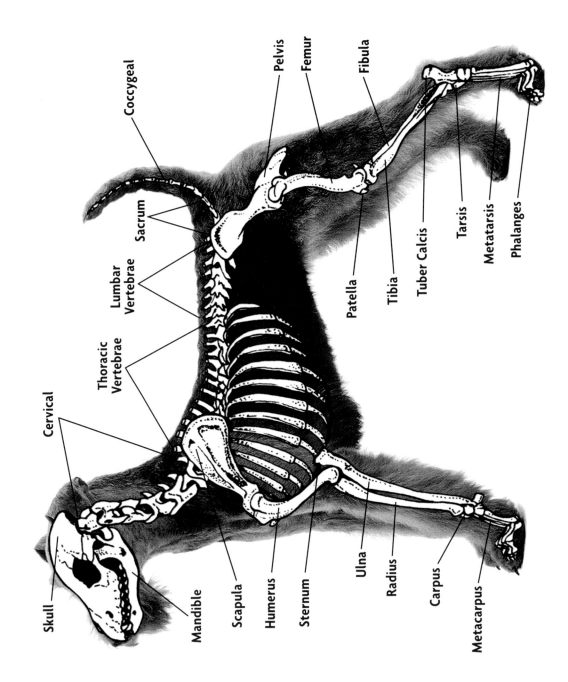

Coccygeal

Pelvis

Femur

Fibula

Sacrum

Tarsis

Metatarsis

Phalanges

Lumbar
Vertebrae

Patella

Tibia

Tuber Calcis

Thoracic
Vertebrae

Cervical

Skull

Mandible

Scapula

Humerus

Sternum

Ulna

Radius

Carpus

Metacarpus

Skeletal Structure of the Airedale Terrier

nourished. For these reasons, a visit to the veterinary surgeon who cared for the dam (mother) is recommended. The dam can pass on disease resistance to her puppies, which can last for eight to ten weeks. She can also pass on parasites and many infections. That's why you should visit the veterinary surgeon who cared for the dam.

VACCINATION SCHEDULING

Most vaccinations are given by injection and should only be done by a veterinary surgeon. Both he and you should keep a record of the date of the injection, the identification of the vaccine and the amount given. Some vets give a first vaccination at eight weeks, but most dog breeders prefer the course not to commence until about ten weeks because of negating any antibodies passed on by the dam. The vaccination scheduling is usually based on a 15-day cycle. You must take your vet's advice as to when to vaccinate as this may differ according to the vaccine used. Most vaccinations immunize your puppy against viruses.

The usual vaccines contain immunizing doses of several different viruses such as distemper, parvovirus, parainfluenza and hepatitis. There are other vaccines available when the puppy is at risk. You should rely upon professional advice. This is

DID YOU KNOW?

Your veterinary surgeon will probably recommend that your puppy be vaccinated before you take him outside. There are airborne diseases, parasite eggs in the grass and unexpected visits from other dogs that might be dangerous to your puppy's health.

especially true for the booster-shot programme. Most vaccination programmes require a booster when the puppy is a year old and once a year thereafter. In some cases, circumstances may require more or less frequent immunizations. Kennel cough, more formally known as tracheobronchitis, is treated with a vaccine that is sprayed into the dog's nostrils. Kennel cough is usually included in routine vaccination, but this is often not so effective as for other major diseases.

WEANING TO FIVE MONTHS OLD

Puppies should be weaned by the time they are about two months old. A puppy that remains for at least eight weeks with its mother and litter mates usually adapts better to other dogs and people later in its life.

Some new owners have their puppy examined by a veterinary surgeon immediately, which is a good idea. Vaccination programmes usually begin when the puppy is very young.

The puppy will have its teeth examined and have its skeletal conformation and general health checked prior to certification by the veterinary surgeon. Puppies in certain breeds have problems with their kneecaps, eye cataracts and other eye problems, heart murmurs and undescended testicles. They may also have personality problems and your veterinary surgeon might have training in temperament evaluation.

FIVE MONTHS TO ONE YEAR OF AGE

Unless you intend to breed or show your dog, neutering the puppy at six months of age is recommended. Discuss this with your veterinary surgeon; most professionals advise neutering the puppy. Neutering has proven to be extremely beneficial to both male and female puppies. Besides eliminating the possibility of pregnancy, it inhibits (but does not prevent) breast cancer in bitches and prostate cancer in male dogs. Under no circumstances should a bitch be spayed prior to her first season.

Your veterinary surgeon should provide your puppy with a thorough dental evaluation at six months of age, ascertaining whether all the permanent teeth have erupted properly. A home dental care regimen should be initiated at six months, including brushing weekly and providing good dental devices (such as nylon bones). Regular dental care promotes healthy teeth, fresh breath and a longer life.

ONE TO SEVEN YEARS

Once a year, your grown dog should visit the vet for an examination and vaccination boosters. Some vets recommend blood tests, thyroid level check and dental evaluation to accompany these annual visits. A thorough clinical evaluation by the vet can provide critical background information for your dog. Blood tests are often performed at one year of age, and dental examinations around the third or fourth birthday. In the long run, quality preventive care for your pet can save money, teeth and lives.

SKIN PROBLEMS IN AIREDALE TERRIERS

Veterinary surgeons are consulted by dog owners for skin problems more than any other group of diseases or maladies. Dogs' skin is almost as sensitive as human skin and both suffer almost the same ailments (though the occurrence of acne in dogs is rare!). For this reason, veterinary dermatology has developed into a speciality practised by many veterinary surgeons.

Since many skin problems have visual symptoms that are almost identical, it requires the

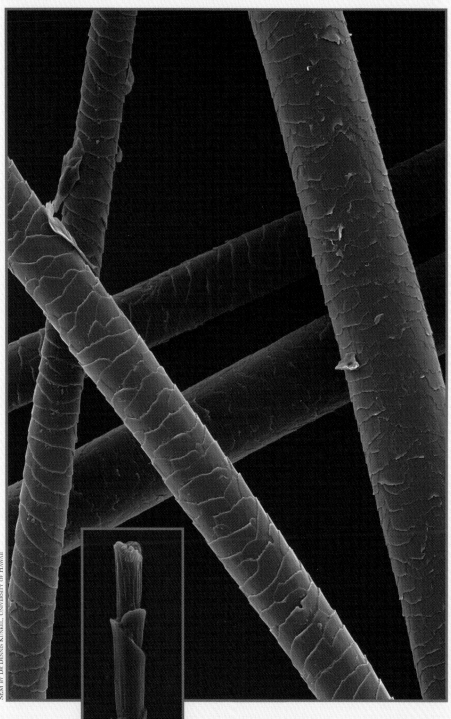

Normal hairs of a dog enlarged 200 times original size. The cuticle (outer covering) is clean and healthy. Unlike human hair that grows from the base, a dog's hair also grows from the end, as shown in the inset. Scanning electron micrographs by Dr Dennis Kunkel, University of Hawaii.

HEALTH AND VACCINATION SCHEDULE

Age in Weeks:	6th	8th	10th	12th	14th	16th	20-24th	1 yr
Worm Control	✔	✔	✔	✔	✔	✔	✔	
Neutering								✔
Heartworm*		✔		✔		✔	✔	
Parvovirus	✔		✔		✔		✔	✔
Distemper		✔		✔		✔		✔
Hepatitis		✔		✔		✔		✔
Leptospirosis								✔
Parainfluenza	✔		✔		✔			✔
Dental Examination		✔					✔	✔
Complete Physical		✔					✔	✔
Coronavirus				✔			✔	✔
Kennel Cough	✔							
Hip Dysplasia								✔
Rabies*							✔	

Vaccinations are not instantly effective. It takes about two weeks for the dog's immunization system to develop antibodies. Most vaccinations require annual booster shots. Your veterinary surgeon should guide you in this regard.
*Not applicable in the United Kingdom

skill of an experienced veterinary dermatologist to identify and cure many of the more severe skin disorders. Pet shops sell many treatments for skin problems but most of the treatments are directed at symptoms and not the underlying problem(s). If your dog is suffering from a skin disorder, you should seek professional assistance as quickly as possible. As with all diseases, the earlier a problem is identified and treated, the more successful is the cure.

HEREDITARY SKIN DISORDERS
Veterinary dermatologists are currently researching a number of skin disorders that are believed to have a hereditary basis. These inherited diseases are transmitted by both parents, who appear (phenotypically) normal but have a recessive gene for the disease, meaning that they carry, but are not affected by, the disease. These diseases pose serious problems to breeders because in some instances there is no method of identifying carriers. Often the secondary diseases associated with these skin conditions are even more debilitating than the disorder itself, including cancers and respiratory problems; others can be lethal.

Among the hereditary skin

disorders, for which the mode of inheritance is known, are: acrodermatitis, cutaneous asthenia (Ehlers-Danlos syndrome), sebaceous adenitis, cyclic hematopoiesis, dermato-myositis, IgA deficiency, colour dilution alopecia and nodular dermatofibrosis. Some of these disorders are limited to one or two breeds and others affect a large number of breeds. All inherited diseases must be diagnosed and treated by a veterinary specialist.

PARASITE BITES
Many of us are allergic to insect bites. The bites itch, erupt and may even become infected. Dogs have the same reaction to fleas, ticks and/or mites. When an insect lands on you, you have the chance to whisk it away with your hand. Unfortunately, when our dog is bitten by a flea, tick or mite, it can only scratch it away or bite it. By the time the dog has been bitten, the parasite has done some of its damage. It may also have laid eggs to cause further

DISEASE REFERENCE CHART

	What is it?	What causes it?	Symptoms
Leptospirosis	Severe disease that affects the internal organs; can be spread to people.	A bacterium, which is often carried by rodents, that enters through mucous membranes and spreads quickly throughout the body.	Range from fever, vomiting and loss of appetite in less severe cases to shock, irreversible kidney damage and possibly death in most severe cases.
Rabies	Potentially deadly virus that infects warm-blooded mammals. Not seen in United Kingdom.	Bite from a carrier of the virus, mainly wild animals.	1st stage: dog exhibits change in behaviour, fear. 2nd stage: dog's behaviour becomes more aggressive. 3rd stage: loss of coordination, trouble with bodily functions.
Parvovirus	Highly contagious virus, potentially deadly.	Ingestion of the virus, which is usually spread through the faeces of infected dogs.	Most common: severe diarrhoea. Also vomiting, fatigue, lack of appetite.
Kennel cough	Contagious respiratory infection.	Combination of types of bacteria and virus. Most common: *Bordetella bronchiseptica* bacteria and parainfluenza virus.	Chronic cough.
Distemper	Disease primarily affecting respiratory and nervous system.	Virus that is related to the human measles virus.	Mild symptoms such as fever, lack of appetite and mucous secretion progress to evidence of brain damage, 'hard pad.'
Hepatitis	Virus primarily affecting the liver.	Canine adenovirus type I (CAV-1). Enters system when dog breathes in particles.	Lesser symptoms include listlessness, diarrhoea, vomiting. More severe symptoms include 'blue-eye' (clumps of virus in eye).
Coronavirus	Virus resulting in digestive problems.	Virus is spread through infected dog's faeces.	Stomach upset evidenced by lack of appetite, vomiting, diarrhoea.

people as well as dogs. The symptoms are variable and may affect the kidneys, bones, blood chemistry and skin. It can be fatal to both dogs and humans, though it is not thought to be transmissible. It is usually successfully treated with cortisone, prednisone or similar corticosteroid, but extensive use of these drugs can have harmful side effects.

AIRBORNE ALLERGIES

An interesting allergy is pollen allergy. Humans have hay fever, rose fever and other fevers with which they suffer during the pollinating season. Many dogs suffer the same allergies. When the pollen count is high, your dog might suffer but don't expect them to sneeze and have runny noses like humans. Dogs react to pollen allergies the same way they react to fleas—

problems in the near future. The itching from parasite bites is probably due to the saliva injected into the site when the parasite sucks the dog's blood.

AUTO-IMMUNE SKIN CONDITIONS

Auto-immune skin conditions are commonly referred to as being allergic to yourself, while allergies are usually inflammatory reactions to an outside stimulus. Auto-immune diseases cause serious damage to the tissues that are involved.

The best known auto-immune disease is lupus, which affects

they scratch and bite themselves.

Dogs, like humans, can be tested for allergens. Discuss the testing with your veterinary dermatologist.

FOOD PROBLEMS

FOOD ALLERGIES

Dogs are allergic to many foods that are best-sellers and highly recommended by breeders and veterinary surgeons. Changing the brand of food that you buy may not eliminate the problem if the element to which the dog is allergic is contained in the new brand.

Recognising a food allergy is difficult. Humans vomit or have rashes when they eat a food to which they are allergic. Dogs neither vomit nor (usually) develop a rash. They react in the same manner as they do to an airborne or flea allergy: they itch, scratch and bite. This makes the diagnosis extremely difficult. While pollen allergies and parasite bites are usually seasonal, food allergies are year-round problems.

FOOD INTOLERANCE

Food intolerance is the inability of the dog to completely digest certain foods. Puppies that may have done very well on their mother's milk may not do well on cow's milk. The rest of this food

intolerance may be loose bowels, passing gas and stomach pains. These are the only obvious symptoms of food intolerance and that makes diagnosis difficult.

TREATING FOOD PROBLEMS

It is possible to handle food allergies and food intolerance yourself. Put your dog on a diet that it has never had. Obviously if it has never eaten this new food it

Dental Health

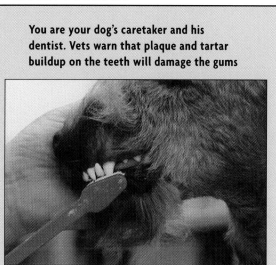

You are your dog's caretaker and his dentist. Vets warn that plaque and tartar buildup on the teeth will damage the gums and allow bacteria to enter the dog's bloodstream, causing serious damage to the animal's vital organs. Studies show that over 50 percent of dogs have some form of gum disease before age three. Daily or weekly tooth cleaning (with a brush or soft gauze pad wipes) can add years to your dog's life.

PET ADVANTAGES

If you do not intend to show or breed your new puppy, your veterinary surgeon will probably recommend that you spay your female or neuter your male. Some people believe neutering leads to weight gain, but if you feed and exercise your dog properly, this is easily avoided. Spaying or neutering can actually have many positive outcomes, such as:

• training becomes easier, as the dog focuses less on the urge to mate and more on you!

• females are protected from unplanned pregnancy as well as ovarian and uterine cancers.

• males are guarded from testicular tumours and have a reduced risk of developing prostate cancer.

Talk to your vet regarding the right age to spay/neuter and other aspects of the procedure.

ingredient cured the problem. You still must find a suitable diet and ascertain which ingredient in the old diet was objectionable. This is most easily done by adding ingredients to the new diet one at a time. Let the dog stay on the modified diet for a month before you add another ingredient. Eventually, you will determine the ingredient that caused the adverse reaction.

An alternative method is to study the ingredients in the diet to which your dog is allergic or intolerant. Identify the main ingredient in this diet and eliminate the main ingredient by buying a different food that does not have that ingredient. Keep experimenting until the symptoms disappear after one month on the new diet.

can't have been allergic or intolerant of it. Start with a single ingredient that is not in the dog's diet at the present time. Ingredients like chopped beef or fish are common in dog's diets, so try something more exotic like rabbit, pheasant or even just vegetables. Keep the dog on this diet (with no additives) for a month. If the symptoms of food allergy or intolerance disappear, chances are your dog has a food allergy.

Don't think that the single

KNOW WHEN TO POSTPONE A VACCINATION

While the visit to the vet is costly, it is never advisable to update a vaccination when visiting with a sick or pregnant dog. Vaccinations should be avoided for all elderly dogs. If your dog is showing the signs of any illness or any medical condition, no matter how serious or mild, including skin irritations, do not vaccinate. Likewise, a lame dog should never be vaccinated; any dog undergoing surgery, or a dog on any immunosuppressant drugs should not be vaccinated until fully recovered.

First Aid at a Glance

Burns
Place the affected area under cool water; use ice if only a small area is burnt.

Bee/Insect bites
Apply ice to relieve swelling; antihistamine dosed properly.

Animal bites
Clean any bleeding area; apply pressure until bleeding subsides; go to the vet.

Spider bites
Use cold compress and a pressurised pack to inhibit venom's spreading.

Antifreeze poisoning
Induce vomiting with hydrogen peroxide. Seek *immediate* veterinary help!

Fish hooks
Removal best handled by vet; hook must be cut in order to remove.

Snake bites
Pack ice around bite; contact vet quickly; identify snake for proper antivenin.

Car accident
Move dog from roadway with blanket; seek veterinary aid.

Shock
Calm the dog, keep him warm; seek immediate veterinary help.

Nosebleed
Apply cold compress to the nose; apply pressure to any visible abrasion.

Bleeding
Apply pressure above the area; treat wound by applying a cotton pack.

Heat stroke
Submerge dog in cold bath; cool down with fresh air and water; go to the vet.

Frostbite/Hypothermia
Warm the dog with a warm bath, electric blankets or hot water bottles.

Abrasions
Clean the wound and wash out thoroughly with fresh water; apply antiseptic.

!! *Remember: an injured dog may attempt to bite a helping hand from fear and confusion. Always muzzle the dog before trying to offer assistance.* !!

A scanning electron micrograph (S. E. M.) of a dog flea, *Ctenocephalides canis*.

S. E. M. BY DR DENNIS KINKEL, UNIVERSITY OF HAWAII

Magnified head of a dog flea, *Ctenocephalides canis*.

S. E. M. BY DR DENNIS KINKEL, UNIVERSITY OF HAWAII

A male dog flea, *Ctenocephalides canis*.

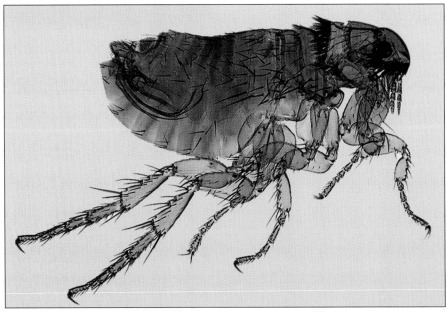

PHOTO BY JEAN CLAUDE REVY/PHOTOTAKE.

EXTERNAL PARASITES

Of all the problems to which dogs are prone, none is more well known and frustrating than fleas. Flea infestation is relatively simple to cure but difficult to prevent. Parasites that are harboured inside the body are a bit more difficult to eradicate but they are easier to control.

FLEAS

To control a flea infestation you have to understand the flea's life cycle. Fleas are often thought of as a summertime problem but centrally heated homes have changed the patterns and fleas can be found at any time of the year. The most effective method of flea control is a two-stage approach:

DID YOU KNOW?
Flea-killers are poisonous. You should not spray these toxic chemicals on areas of a dog's body that he licks, on his genitals or on his face. Flea killers taken internally are a better answer, but check with your vet in case internal therapy is not advised for your dog.

one stage to kill the adult fleas, and the other to control the development of pre-adult fleas. Unfortunately, no single active ingredient is effective against all stages of the life cycle.

LIFE CYCLE STAGES
During its life, a flea will pass through four life stages: egg, larva, pupa and adult. The adult stage is the most visible and irritating stage of the flea life cycle and this is why the majority of flea-control products concentrate on this stage. The fact is that adult fleas account for only 1% of the total flea population, and the other 99% exist in pre-adult stages, i.e. eggs, larvae and pupae. The pre-adult stages are barely visible to the naked eye.

THE LIFE CYCLE OF THE FLEA
Eggs are laid on the dog, usually in quantities of about 20 or 30, several times a day. The female adult flea must have a blood meal before each egg-laying session. When first laid, the eggs will cling to the dog's fur, as the eggs are still moist. However, they will quickly dry out and fall from the dog, especially if the dog moves around or scratches. Many eggs will fall off in the dog's favourite area or an area in which he spends a lot of time, such as his bed.

Once the eggs fall from the dog onto the carpet or furniture, they will hatch into larvae. This takes from one to ten days. Larvae are not particularly mobile, and will usually travel only a few inches from where they hatch. However, they do have a tendency to move

A Look at Fleas

**Fleas have been around for millions of years and have adapted to changing host animals.
They are able to go through a complete life cycle in less than one month or they can extend their lives to almost two years by remaining as pupae or cocoons. They do not need blood or any other food for up to 20 months.**

They have been measured as being able to jump 300,000 times and can jump 150 times their length in any direction including straight up. Those are just a few of the reasons why they are so successful in infesting a dog!

ILLUSTRATION COURTESY OF BAYER VITAL GMBH & CO. KG

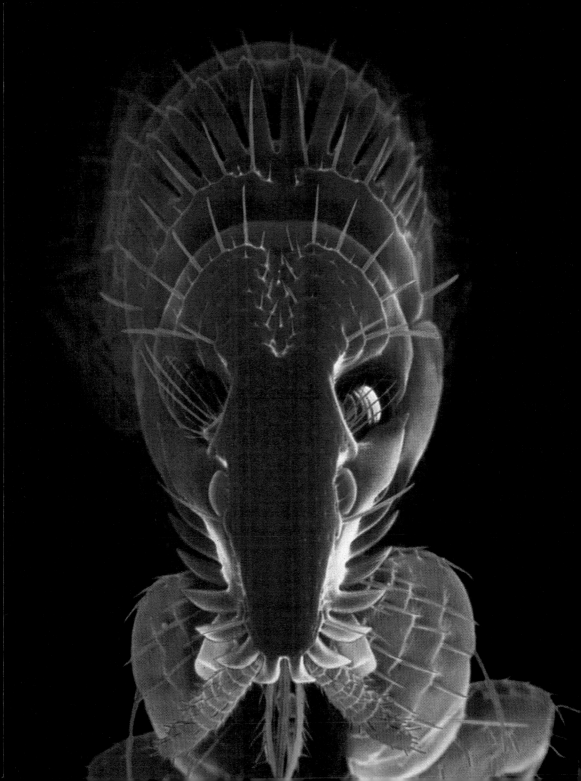

away from light and heavy traffic—under furniture and behind doors are common places to find high quantities of flea larvae.

The flea larvae feed on dead organic matter, including adult flea faeces, until they are ready to change into adult fleas. Fleas will usually remain as larvae for around seven days. After this period, the larvae will pupate into protective pupae. While inside the pupae, the larvae will undergo metamorphosis and change into adult fleas. This can take as little time as a few days, but the adult fleas can remain inside the pupae waiting to hatch for up to two years. The pupae are signalled to hatch by certain stimuli, such as physical pressure—the pupae's being stepped on, heat from an animal lying on the pupae or increased carbon dioxide levels and vibrations—indicating that a suitable host is available.

Once hatched, the adult flea must feed within a few days. Once the adult flea finds a host, it will not leave voluntarily. It only becomes dislodged by grooming or

DID YOU KNOW?
Never mix flea control products without first consulting your veterinary surgeon. Some products can become toxic when combined with others and can cause serious or fatal consequences.

EN GARDE: CATCHING FLEAS OFF GUARD
Consider the following ways to arm yourself against fleas:
• Add a small amount of pennyroyal or eucalyptus oil to your dog's bath. These natural remedies repel fleas.
• Supplement your dog's food with fresh garlic (minced or grated) and a hearty amount of brewer's yeast, both of which ward off fleas.
• Use a flea comb on your dog daily. Submerge fleas in a cup of bleach to kill them quickly.
• Confine the dog to only a few rooms to limit the spread of fleas in the home.
• Vacuum daily . . . and get all of the crevices! Dispose of the bag every few days until the problem is under control.
• Wash your dog's bedding daily. Cover cushions where your dog sleeps with towels, and wash the towels often.

the host animal's scratching. The adult flea will remain on the host for the duration of its life unless forcibly removed.

TREATING THE ENVIRONMENT AND THE DOG
Treating fleas should be a two-pronged attack. First, the environment needs to be treated; this includes carpets and furniture, especially the dog's bedding and

Opposite page: A scanning electron micrograph of a dog or cat flea, *Ctenocephalides*, magnified more than 100x. This image has been colourized for effect.

The Life Cycle of the Flea

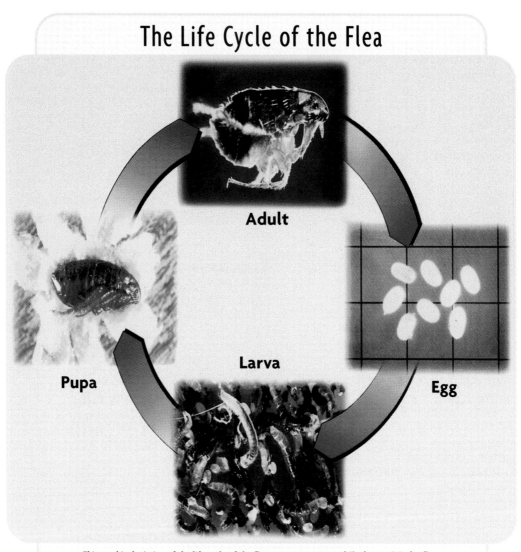

Adult

Pupa

Larva

Egg

This graphic depiction of the life cycle of the flea appears courtesy of Fleabusters®, R$_x$ for fleas.

areas underneath furniture. The environment should be treated with a household spray containing an Insect Growth Regulator (IGR) and an insecticide to kill the adult fleas. Most IGRs are effective against eggs and larvae; they actually mimic the fleas' own hormones and stop the eggs and larvae from developing into adult fleas. There are currently no treatments available to attack the pupa stage of the life cycle, so the adult insecticide is used to kill the newly hatched adult fleas before

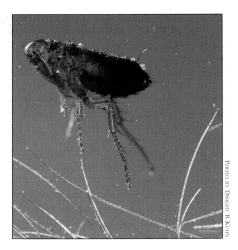

Photo by Dwight R Kuhn

TICKS AND MITES

Though not as common as fleas, ticks and mites are found all over the tropical and temperate world. They don't bite, like fleas; they harpoon. They dig their sharp proboscis (nose) into the dog's skin and drink the blood. Their only food and drink is dog's blood. Dogs can get Lyme disease, Rocky Mountain spotted fever (normally

they find a host. Most IGRs are active for many months, whilst adult insecticides are only active for a few days.

When treating with a household spray, it is a good idea to vacuum before applying the product. This stimulates as many pupae as possible to hatch into adult fleas. The vacuum cleaner should also be treated with a flea treatment to prevent the eggs and larvae that have been hoovered into the vacuum bag from hatching.

The second stage of treatment is to apply an adult insecticide to the dog. Traditionally, this would be in the form of a collar or a spray, but more recent innovations include digestible insecticides that poison the fleas when they ingest the dog's blood. Alternatively, there are drops that, when placed on the back of the animal's neck, spread throughout the fur and skin to kill adult fleas.

FLEA CONTROL

Two types of products should be used when treating fleas—a product to treat the pet and a product to treat the home. Adult fleas represent less than 1% of the flea population. The pre-adult fleas (eggs, larvae and pupae) represent more than 99% of the flea population and are found in the environment; it is in the case of pre-adult fleas that products containing an Insect Growth Regulator (IGR) should be used in the home.

IGRs are a new class of compounds used to prevent the development of insects. They do not kill the insect outright, but instead use the insect's biology against it to stop it from completing its growth. Products that contain methoprene are the world's first and leading IGRs. Used to control fleas and other insects, this type of IGR will stop flea larvae from developing and protect the house for up to seven months.

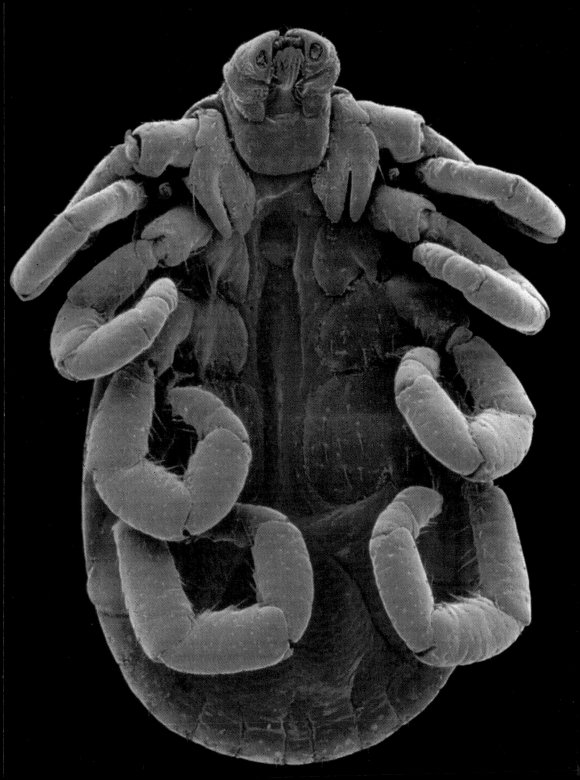

found in the US only), paralysis and many other diseases from ticks and mites. They may live where fleas are found and they like to hide in cracks or seams in walls wherever dogs live. They are controlled the same way fleas are controlled.

The dog tick, *Dermacentor variabilis*, may well be the most common dog tick in many geographical areas, especially those areas where the climate is hot and humid.

Most dog ticks have life expectancies of a week to six

Beware the Deer Tick

The great outdoors may be fun for your dog, but it also is a home to dangerous ticks. Deer ticks carry a bacterium known as *Borrelia burgdorferi* and are most active in the autumn and spring. When infections are caught early, penicillin and tetracycline are effective antibiotics, but if left untreated the bacteria may cause neurological, kidney and cardiac problems as well as long-term trouble with walking and painful joints.

ILLUSTRATION COURTESY OF BAYER VITAL GMBH & CO. KG

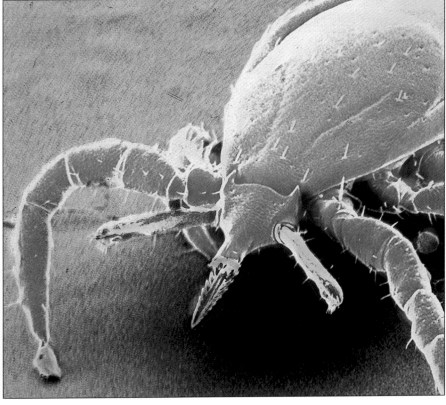

S. E. M. BY DR ANDREW SPIELMAN/PHOTOTAKE

A deer tick, the carrier of Lyme disease. This magnified micrograph has been colourized for effect.

Opposite page: The dog tick, *Dermacentor variabilis*, is probably the most common tick found on dogs. Look at the strength in its eight legs! No wonder it's hard to detach them.

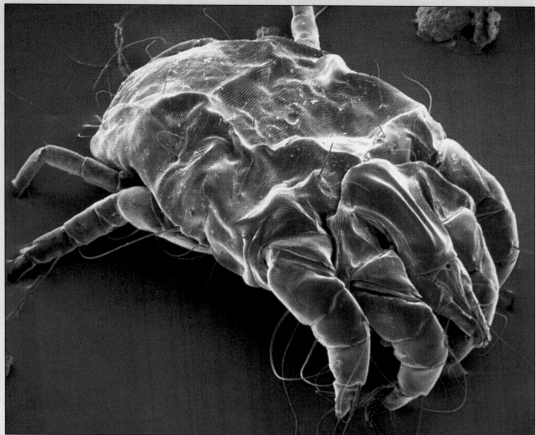

Above:
The mange mite,
Psoroptes bovis.

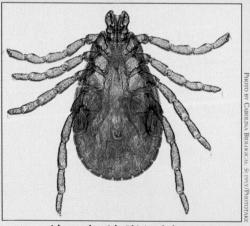

A brown dog tick, *Rhipicephalus sanguineus*, is
an uncommon but annoying tick found on dogs.

Human lice look like dog lice;
the two are closely related.

months, depending upon climatic conditions. They can neither jump nor fly, but they can crawl slowly and can range up to 5 metres (16 feet) to reach a sleeping or unsuspecting dog.

MANGE

Mites cause a skin irritation called mange. Some are contagious, like *Cheyletiella*, ear mites, scabies and chiggers. Mites that cause ear-mite infestations are usually controlled with Lindane, which can only be administered by a vet, followed by Tresaderm at home.

It is essential that your dog be treated for mange as quickly as possible because some forms of mange are transmissible to people.

INTERNAL PARASITES

Most animals—fishes, birds and mammals, including dogs and humans—have worms and other parasites that live inside their bodies. According to Dr Herbert R Axelrod, the fish pathologist, there are two kinds of parasites: dumb and smart. The smart parasites live in peaceful cooper-ation with their hosts (symbiosis), while the dumb parasites kill their host. Most of the worm infections are relatively easy to control. If they are not controlled they weaken the host dog to the point that other medical problems occur, but they are not dumb parasites.

ROUNDWORMS

The roundworms that infect dogs are scientifically known as *Toxocara canis*. They live in the dog's intestine. The worms shed eggs continually. It has been estimated that a dog produces about 150 grammes of faeces every day. Each gramme of faeces averages 10,000–12,000 eggs of roundworms. There are no known areas in which dogs roam that do not contain roundworm eggs. The greatest danger of roundworms is that they infect people too! It is

DEWORMING

Ridding your puppy of worms is VERY IMPORTANT because certain worms that puppies carry, such as tapeworms and roundworms, can infect humans.

Breeders initiate a deworming programme at or about four weeks of age. The routine is repeated every two or three weeks until the puppy is three months old. The breeder from whom you obtained your puppy should provide you with the complete details of the deworming programme.

Your veterinary surgeon can prescribe and monitor the programme of deworming for you. The usual programme is treating the puppy every 15–20 days until the puppy is positively worm free.

It is advised that you only treat your puppy with drugs that are recommended professionally.

wise to have your dog tested regularly for roundworms.

Pigs also have roundworm infections that can be passed to humans and dogs. The typical roundworm parasite is called *Ascaris lumbricoides.*

HOOKWORMS

The worm *Ancylostoma caninum* is commonly called the dog hookworm. It is dangerous to humans and cats. It also has teeth by which it attaches itself to the intestines of the dog. It changes the site of its attachment about six times a day and the dog loses blood from each detachment, possibly causing iron-deficiency anaemia. Hookworms are easily purged from the dog with many medications. Milbemycin oxime,

ROUNDWORM

Average size dogs can pass 1,360,000 roundworm eggs every day.

For example, if there were only 1 million dogs in the world, the world would be saturated with 1,300 metric tonnes of dog faeces.

These faeces would contain 15,000,000,000 roundworm eggs.

7–31% of home gardens and children's play boxes in the U. S. contain roundworm eggs.

Flushing dog's faeces down the toilet is not a safe practice because the usual sewage treatments do not destroy roundworm eggs.

Infected puppies start shedding roundworm eggs at 3 weeks of age. They can be infected by their mother's milk.

The roundworm, *Rhabditis.* The roundworm can infect both dogs and humans.

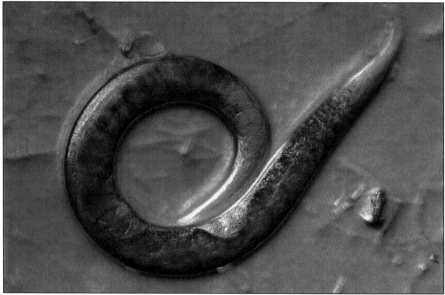

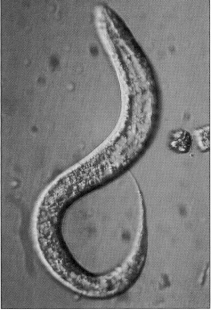

PHOTO BY C. JAMES WEBB/PHOTOTAKE

PHOTO BY DWIGHT R KUHN.

Left:
The infective
stage of the
hookworm larva.

Right:
Male and female
hookworms,
*Ancylostoma
caninum*, are
uncommonly
found in pet or
show dogs in
Britain.
Hookworms may
infect other dogs
that have exposure
to grasslands.

which also serves as a heartworm preventative in Collies, can be used for this purpose.

In Britain the 'temperate climate' hookworm (*Uncinaria stenocephala*) is rarely found in pet or show dogs, but can occur in

hunting packs, racing Greyhounds and sheepdogs because the worms can be prevalent wherever dogs are exercised regularly on grassland.

TAPEWORMS
There are many species of tapeworms. They are carried by fleas! The dog eats the flea and starts the tapeworm cycle. Humans can also be infected with tapeworms, so don't eat fleas! Fleas are so small that your dog could pass them onto your hands, your plate or your food and thus make it possible for you to ingest a flea which is carrying tapeworm eggs.

While tapeworm infection is not life threatening in dogs (smart parasite!), it can be the cause of a

DID YOU KNOW?
Never allow your dog to swim in polluted water or public areas where water quality can be suspect. Even perfectly clear water can harbour parasites, many of which can cause serious to fatal illnesses in canines. Areas inhabited by waterfowl and other wildlife are especially dangerous.

141

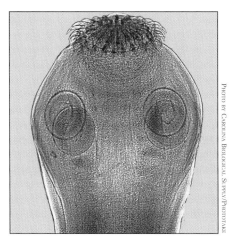

The head and rostellum (the round prominence on the scolex) of a tapeworm, which infects dogs and humans.

PHOTO BY CAROLINA BIOLOGICAL SUPPLY/PHOTOTAKE

very serious liver disease for humans. About 50 percent of the humans infected with *Echinococcus multilocularis*, a type of tapeworm that causes alveolar hydatis, perish.

HEARTWORMS

Heartworms are thin, extended worms up to 30 cms (12 ins) long which live in a dog's heart and the major blood vessels surrounding it. Dogs may have up to 200 worms. Symptoms may be loss of energy, loss of appetite, coughing, the development of a pot belly and anaemia.

Heartworms are transmitted by mosquitoes. The mosquito drinks the blood of an infected dog and takes in larvae with the blood. The larvae, called microfilaria, develop within the body of the mosquito and are passed on to the next dog bitten after the larvae mature. It takes two to three weeks for the

---

TAPEWORM

Humans, rats, squirrels, foxes, coyotes, wolves, mixed breeds of dogs and purebred dogs are all susceptible to tapeworm infection. Except in humans, tapeworms are usually not a fatal infection.

Infected individuals can harbour a thousand parasitic worms.

Tapeworms have two sexes—male and female (many other worms have only one sex—male and female in the same worm).

If dogs eat infected rats or mice, they get the tapeworm disease.

One month after attaching to a dog's intestine, the worm starts shedding eggs. These eggs are infective immediately.

Infective eggs can live for a few months without a host animal.

Roundworms, whipworms and hookworms are just a few of the other commonly known worms that infect dogs.

---

larvae to develop to the infective stage within the body of the mosquito. Dogs should be treated at about six weeks of age, and maintained on a prophylactic dose given monthly.

Blood testing for heartworms is not necessarily indicative of how seriously your dog is infected. This is a dangerous disease. Although heartworm is a problem for dogs in America, Australia, Asia and Central Europe, dogs in the United Kingdom are not currently affected by heartworm.

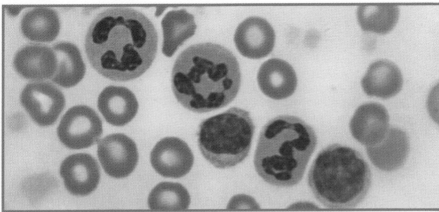

Magnified heartworm larvae, *Dirofilaria immitis.*

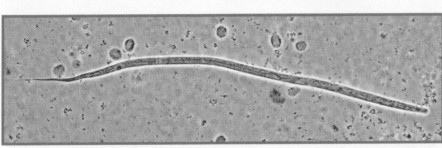

The heartworm, *Dirofilaria immitis.*

The heart of a dog infected with canine heartworm, *Dirofilaria immitis.*

HOMEOPATHY:
an alternative to medicine

'Less is Most'

Using this principle, the strength of a homeopathic remedy is measured by the number of serial dilutions that were undertaken to create it. The greater the number of serial dilutions, the greater the strength of the homeopathic remedy. The potency of a remedy that has been made by making a dilution of 1 part in 100 parts (or 1/100) is 1c or 1cH. If this remedy is subjected to a series of further dilutions, each one being 1/100, a more dilute and stronger remedy is produced. If the remedy is diluted in this way six times, it is called 6c or 6cH. A dilution of 6c is 1 part in 1000,000,000,000. In general, higher potencies in more frequent doses are better for acute symptoms and lower potencies in more infrequent doses are more useful for chronic, long-standing problems.

CURING OUR DOGS NATURALLY

Holistic medicine means treating the whole animal as a unique, perfect living being. Generally, holistic treatments do not suppress the symptoms that the body naturally produces, as do most medications prescribed by conventional doctors and vets. Holistic methods seek to cure disease by regaining balance and harmony in the patient's environment. Some of these methods include use of nutritional therapy, herbs, flower essences, aromatherapy, acupuncture, massage, chiropractic, and, of course the most popular holistic approach, homeopathy. Homeopathy is a theory or system of treating illness with small doses of substances which, if administered in larger quantities, would produce the symptoms that the patient already has. This approach is often described as 'like cures like.' Although modern veterinary medicine is geared toward the 'quick fix,' homeopathy relies on the belief that, given the time, the body is able to heal itself and return to its natural, healthy state.

Choosing a remedy to cure a problem in our dogs is the difficult part of homeopathy. Consult with your veterinary surgeon for a professional diagnosis of your dog's symptoms. Often these symptoms require immediate conventional

care. If your vet is willing, and somewhat knowledgeable, you may attempt a homeopathic remedy. Be aware that cortisone prevents homeopathic remedies from working. There are hundreds of possibilities and combinations to cure many problems in dogs, from basic physical problems such as excessive moulting, fleas or other parasites, unattractive doggy odour, bad breath, upset tummy, dry, oily or dull coat, diarrhoea, ear problems or eye discharge (including tears and dry or mucousy matter), to behavioural abnormalities, such as fear of loud noises, habitual licking, poor appetite, excessive barking, obesity and various phobias. From alumina to zincum metallicum, the remedies span the planet and the imagination…from flowers and weeds to chemicals, insect droppings, diesel smoke and volcanic ash.

Using 'Like to Treat Like'

Unlike conventional medicines that suppress symptoms, homeopathic remedies treat illnesses with small doses of substances that, if administered in larger quantities, would produce the symptoms that the patient already has. Whilst the same homeopathic remedy can be used to treat different symptoms in different dogs, here are some interesting remedies and their uses.

Apis Mellifica
(made from honey bee venom) can be used for allergies or to reduce swelling that occurs in acutely infected kidneys.

Diesel Smoke
can be used to help control travel sickness.

Calcarea Fluorica
(made from calcium fluoride which helps harden bone structure) can be useful in treating hard lumps in tissues.

Natrum Muriaticum
(made from common salt, sodium chloride) is useful in treating thin, thirsty dogs.

Nitricum Acidum
(made from nitric acid) is used for symptoms you would expect to see from contact with acids such as lesions, especially where the skin joins the linings of body orifices or openings such as the lips and nostrils.

Symphytum
(made from the herb Knitbone, Symphytum officianale) is used to encourage bones to heal.

Urtica Urens
(made from the common stinging nettle) is used in treating painful, irritating rashes.

HOMEOPATHIC REMEDIES FOR YOUR DOG

Symptom/Ailment	Possible Remedy
ALLERGIES	Apis Mellifica 30c, Astacus Fluviatilis 6c, Pulsatilla 30c, Urtica Urens 6c
ALOPECIA	Alumina 30c, Lycopodium 30c, Sepia 30c, Thallium 6c
ANAL GLANDS (BLOCKED)	Hepar Sulphuris Calcareum 30c, Sanicula 6c, Silicea 6c
ARTHRITIS	Rhus Toxicodendron 6c, Bryonia Alba 6c
CATARACT	Calcarea Carbonica 6c, Conium Maculatum 6c, Phosphorus 30c, Silicea 30c
CONSTIPATION	Alumina 6c, Carbo Vegetabilis 30c, Graphites 6c, Nitricum Acidum 30c, Silicea 6c
COUGHING	Aconitum Napellus 6c, Belladonna 30c, Hyoscyamus Niger 30c, Phosphorus 30c
DIARRHOEA	Arsenicum Album 30c, Aconitum Napellus 6c, Chamomilla 30c, Mercurius Corrosivus 30c
DRY EYE	Zincum Metallicum 30c
EAR PROBLEMS	Aconitum Napellus 30c, Belladonna 30c, Hepar Sulphuris 30c, Tellurium 30c, Psorinum 200c
EYE PROBLEMS	Borax 6c, Aconitum Napellus 30c, Graphites 6c, Staphysagria 6c, Thuja Occidentalis 30c
GLAUCOMA	Aconitum Napellus 30c, Apis Mellifica 6c, Phosphorus 30c
HEAT STROKE	Belladonna 30c, Gelsemium Sempervirens 30c, Sulphur 30c
HICCOUGHS	Cinchona Deficinalis 6c
HIP DYSPLASIA	Colocynthis 6c, Rhus Toxicodendron 6c, Bryonia Alba 6c
INCONTINENCE	Argentum Nitricum 6c, Causticum 30c, Conium Maculatum 30c, Pulsatilla 30c, Sepia 30c
INSECT BITES	Apis Mellifica 30c, Cantharis 30c, Hypericum Perforatum 6c, Urtica Urens 30c
ITCHING	Alumina 30c, Arsenicum Album 30c, Carbo Vegetabilis 30c, Hypericum Perforatum 6c, Mezerium 6c, Sulphur 30c
KENNEL COUGH	Drosera 6c, Ipecacuanha 30c
MASTITIS	Apis Mellifica 30c, Belladonna 30c, Urtica Urens 1m
PATELLAR LUXATION	Gelsemium Sempervirens 6c, Rhus Toxicodendron 6c
PENIS PROBLEMS	Aconitum Napellus 30c, Hepar Sulphuris Calcareum 30c, Pulsatilla 30c, Thuja Occidentalis 6c
PUPPY TEETHING	Calcarea Carbonica 6c, Chamomilla 6c, Phytolacca 6c
TRAVEL SICKNESS	Cocculus 6c, Petroleum 6c

Recognising a Sick Dog

Unlike colicky babies and cranky children, our canine kids cannot tell us when they are feeling ill. Therefore, there are a number of signs that owners can identify to know that their dogs are not feeling well.

**Take note for
physical manifestations such as:**

- unusual, bad odour, including bad breath
- excessive moulting
- wax in the ears, chronic ear irritation
- oily, flaky, dull haircoat
- mucous, tearing or similar discharge in the eyes
- fleas or mites
- mucous in stool, diarrhoea
- sensitivity to petting or handling
- licking at paws, scratching face, etc.

**Keep an eye out for
behavioural changes as well including:**

- lethargy, idleness
- lack of patience or general irritability
- lack of appetite, digestive problems
- phobias (fear of people, loud noises, etc.)
- strange behaviour, suspicion, fear
- coprophagia
- more frequent barking
- whimpering, crying

Get Well Soon

You don't need a DVR or a BVMA to provide good TLC to your sick or recovering dog, but you do need to pay attention to some details that normally wouldn't bother him. The following tips will aid Fido's recovery and get him back on his paws again:

- Keep his space free of irritating smells, like heavy perfumes and air fresheners.
- Rest is the best medicine! Avoid harsh lighting that will prevent your dog from sleeping. Shade him from bright sunlight during the day and dim the lights in the evening.
- Keep the noise level down. Animals are more sensitive to sound when they are sick.

- Be attentive to any necessary temperature adjustments. A dog with a fever needs a cool room and cold liquids. A bitch that is whelping or recovering from surgery will be more comfortable in a warm room, consuming warm liquids and food.
- You wouldn't send a sick child back to school early, so don't rush your dog back into a full routine until he seems absolutely ready.

When you purchased your Airedale Terrier you should have made it clear to the breeder whether you wanted one just as a loveable companion and pet, or if you hoped to be buying a Airedale Terrier with show prospects. No reputable breeder will sell you a young puppy saying that it is definitely of show quality, for so much can go wrong during the early weeks and months of a puppy's development. If you plan to show what you will hopefully have acquired is a puppy with 'show potential.'

To the novice, exhibiting an Airedale Terrier in the show ring may look easy but it takes a lot of hard work and devotion to do top winning at a show such as the prestigious Crufts, not to mention a little luck too!

The first concept that the canine novice learns when watching a dog show is that each breed first competes against members of its own breed. Once the judge has selected the best member of each breed, provided that the show is judged on a Group system, that chosen dog will compete with other dogs in its group. Finally the best of each group will compete for Best in Show and Reserve Best in Show.

The second concept that you must understand is that the dogs are not actually competing against one another. The judge compares each dog against the breed standard, which is a written description of the ideal specimen of the breed. While some early breed standards were indeed based on specific dogs that were famous or popular, many dedicated enthusiasts say that a perfect specimen, described in the standard, has never been bred. Thus the 'perfect' dog never walked into a show ring and, to the woe of dog breeders around the globe, does not exist. Breeders attempt to get as close to this ideal as possible, with every litter, but theoretically the 'perfect' dog is so elusive that it is impossible. (Even if the 'perfect' dog were born, breeders and judges would never agree that it was indeed 'perfect.')

If you are interested in exploring dog shows, your best bet is to join your local breed club. These clubs often host both Championship and Open shows, and sometimes Match meetings and Special Events, all of which could be of interest, even if you are only an onlooker. Clubs also send out newsletters and some organise training days and seminars in order that people may learn more about their chosen breed. To locate the nearest breed club for you, contact The Kennel Club, the ruling body for the British dog world. The Kennel Club governs not only conformation shows but also working trials, obedience trials, agility trials and field trials. The Kennel Club furnishes the rules and regulations for all these events plus general dog registration and other basic requirements of dog ownership. Its annual show called the Crufts Dog Show, held in Birmingham, is the largest benched show in England. Every year around 20,000 of the UK's best dogs qualify to participate in this marvellous show which lasts four days.

The Kennel Club governs many different kinds of shows in Great Britain, Australia, South Africa and beyond. At the most competitive and prestigious of these shows, the Championship Shows, a dog can earn Challenge Certificates, and thereby become a Show Champion or a Champion. A dog must earn three Challenge Certificates under three different judges to earn the prefix of 'Sh Ch' or 'Ch.' Note that some breeds must also qualify in a field trial in order to gain the title of full champion. Challenge Certificates are awarded to a very small percentage of the dogs competing,

Show Quality Shows

While you may purchase a puppy in the hope of having a successful career in the show ring, it is impossible to tell, at eight to ten weeks,

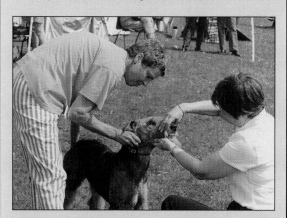

whether your dog will be a contender. Some promising pups end up with minor to serious faults that prevent them from taking home a Best of Breed award, but this certainly does not mean they can't be the best of companions for you and your family. To find out if your potential show dog is show quality, enter him in a match to see how a judge evaluates him. You may also take him back to your breeder as he matures to see what he might advise.

especially as dogs which are already Champions compete with others for these coveted CCs. The number of Challenge Certificates awarded in any one year is based upon the total number of dogs in each breed entered for competition. There are three types of Championship Shows: an all-breed General Championship show for all Kennel-Club-recognised breeds; a Group Championship Show, limited to breeds within one of the groups; and a Breed Show, usually confined to a single breed. The Kennel Club determines which breeds at which Championship Shows will have the opportunity to earn Challenge Certificates (or tickets). Serious exhibitors often will opt not to participate if the tickets are withheld at a particular show. This policy makes earning championships ever more difficult to accomplish.

Open Shows are generally less competitive and are frequently used as 'practice shows' for young dogs. There are hundreds of Open Shows each year that can be invitingly social events and are great first show experiences for the novice. Even if you're considering just watching a show to 'whet' your paws, an Open Show is a great choice.

While Championship and Open Shows are most important for the beginner to understand, there are other types of shows in which the interested dog owner can participate. Training clubs sponsor Matches that can be entered on the day of the show for a nominal fee. In these introductory-level exhibitions, two dogs are pulled out of a hat and 'matched,' the winner of that match goes on to the next round, and eventually only one dog is

left undefeated.

Exemption Shows are much more light-hearted affairs with usually only four pedigree classes and several 'fun' classes, all of which can be entered on the day. Exemption Shows are sometimes held in conjunction with small agricultural shows, and the proceeds must be given to charity. Limited Shows are also available in small number, but entry is restricted to members of the club which hosts the show, although one can usually join the club when making an entry.

Before you actually step into the ring, you would be well advised to sit back and observe the judge's ring procedure. If it is your first time in the ring, do not be over-anxious and run to the front of the line. It is much better to stand back and study how the exhibitor in front of you is performing. The judge asks each handler to 'stand' the dog, hopefully showing the dog off to his best advantage. The judge will observe the dog from a distance and from different angles, approach the dog, check his teeth, overall structure, alertness and muscle tone, as well as consider how well the dog 'conforms' to the standard. Most importantly, the judge will have the exhibitor move the dog around the ring in some pattern that he or she should specify (another advantage to not going first, but always listen since some judges change their directions, and the judge is always right!) Finally the judge will give the dog one last look before moving on to the next exhibitor.

If you are not in the top three at your first show, do not be discouraged. Be patient and consistent and you may eventually find yourself in the winning lineup. Remember that the winners were once in your shoes and have devoted many hours and much money to earn the placement. If you find that your dog is losing every time and never getting a nod, it may be time to consider a different dog sport or just enjoy your Airedale Terrier as a pet.

WORKING TRIALS

Working trials can be entered by any well-trained dog of any breed, not just Gundogs or Working dogs. Many dogs that earn the Kennel Club Good Citizen Dog award choose to participate in a working trial. There are five stakes at both open and championship levels: Companion Dog (CD), Utility Dog (UD), Working Dog (WD), Tracking Dog (TD) and Patrol Dog (PD). As in conformation shows, dogs compete against a standard and if the dog reaches the qualifying mark, it obtains a certificate. Divided into groups, each exercise must be achieved 70 percent in order to qualify. If the dog

Winning the Ticket

Earning a championship at Kennel Club shows is the most difficult in the world. Compared to the United States and Canada where it is

relatively not 'challenging,' collecting three green tickets not only requires much time and effort, it can be very expensive! Challenge Certificates, as the tickets are properly known, are the building blocks of champions—good breeding, good handling, good training and good luck!

achieves 80 percent in the open level, it receives a Certificate of Merit (COM), in the championship level, it receives a Qualifying Certificate. At the CD stake, dogs must participate in four groups, Control, Stay, Agility and Search (Retrieve and Nosework). At the next three levels, UD, WD and TD, there are

NO SHOW

Never show a dog that is sick, lame or recovering from surgery or infection. Not only will this put your own dog under a tremendous amount of stress, but you will also put other dogs at risk of contracting any illness your dog has. Bitches who are in heat will distract and disrupt the performances of males who are competing, and bitches that are pregnant will likely be stressed and exhausted by a long day of showing.

only three groups: Control, Agility and Nosework.

Agility consists of three jumps: a vertical scale up a six-foot wall of planks; a clear jump over a basic three-foot hurdle with a removable top bar; and a long jump across angled planks stretching nine feet.

To earn the UD, WD and TD, dogs must track approximately one-half mile for articles laid from one-half hour to three hours ago. Tracks consist of turns and legs, and fresh ground is used for each participant. The fifth stake, PD, involves teaching manwork, which is not recommended for every breed, although a well-bred Airedale is an excellent candidate.

FIELD TRIALS AND WORKING TESTS

Working tests are frequently used to prepare dogs for field trials, the purpose of which is to heighten the instincts and natural abilities of gundogs. Live game is not used in working tests. Unlike field trials, working tests do not count toward a dog's record at The Kennel Club, though the same judges often oversee working tests. Field trials began in England in 1947 and are only moderately popular among dog folk. While breeders of Working and Gundog breeds concern themselves with the field abilities of their dogs, there is considerably less interest in field trials than dog shows. In order for dogs to become full champions, certain breeds must qualify in the field as well. Upon gaining three CCs in the show ring, the dog is designated a Show Champion (Sh Ch). The title Champion (Ch) requires that the dog gain an award at a field trial, be a 'special qualifier' at a field trial or pass a 'special show dog qualifier' judged by a field trial judge on a shooting day.

AGILITY TRIALS

Agility trials began in the United Kingdom in 1977 and have since spread around the world, especially to the United States, where the sport enjoys strong popularity. The handler directs his dog over an obstacle course that includes jumps (such as those used in the working trials), as well as tyres, the dog walk, weave poles, pipe tunnels, collapsed

TEMPERAMENT PLUS

Although it seems that physical conformation is the only factor considered in the show ring, temperament is also of utmost importance. An aggressive or fearful dog should not be shown, as bad behaviour will not be tolerated and may pose a threat to the judge, other exhibitors, you and your dog.

months old. This dog sport intends to be great fun for dog and owner and interested owners should join a training club that has obstacles and experienced agility handlers who can introduce you and your dog to the 'ropes' (and tyres, tunnels and so on).

FÉDÉRATION CYNOLOGIQUE INTERNATIONALE
Established in 1911, the Fédération Cynologique Internationale (FCI) represents the 'world kennel club.' This international body

tunnels, etc. The Kennel Club requires that dogs not be trained for agility until they are 12

Winning the Terrier Group at the prestigious Crufts Dog Show is Airedale Terrier Ch Jokyl This is My Song. This victory took place in March 1996.

Show Ring Etiquette

Just as with anything else, there is a certain etiquette to the show ring that can only be learned through experience. Showing your dog can be quite intimidating to you as a novice when it seems as if everyone else knows what they are doing. You can familiarise yourself with ring procedure beforehand by taking a class to prepare you and your dog for

conformation showing or by talking with an experienced handler. When you are in the ring, listen and pay attention to the judge and follow his/her directions. Remember, even the most skilled handlers had to start somewhere. Keep it up and you too will become a proficient handler before too long!

included only four European nations: France, Holland, Austria and Belgium (which remains its headquarters), the organisation today embraces nations on six continents and recognises well over 300 breeds of purebred dog. There are three titles attainable through the FCI: the International Champion, which is the most prestigious; the International Beauty Champion, which is based on aptitude certificates in different countries; and the International Trial Champion, which is based on achievement in obedience trials in different countries. Quarantine laws in England and Australia prohibit most of their exhibitors from entering FCI shows. The rest of the Continent does participate in these impressive canine spectacles, the largest of which is the World Dog Show, hosted in a different country each year. FCI sponsors both national and international shows. The hosting country determines the judging system and breed standards are always based on the breed's country of origin.

The FCI is divided into ten 'Groups.' At the World Dog Show, the following 'Classes' are offered for each breed: Puppy Class (6–9 months), Youth Class (9–18 months), Open Class (15 months or older) and Champion Class. A dog can be awarded a classification of Excellent, Very Good,

brings uniformity to the breeding, judging and showing of purebred dogs. Although the FCI originally

Good, Sufficient and Not Sufficient. Puppies can be awarded classifications of Very Promising, Promising or Not Promising. Four placements are made in each class. After all sexes and classes are judged, a Best of Breed is selected. Other special groups and classes may also be shown. Each exhibitor showing a dog receives a written evaluation from the judge.

Besides the World Dog Show, you can exhibit your dog at speciality shows held by different breed clubs. Speciality shows may have their own regulations.

PRACTISE AT HOME

If you have decided to show your dog, you must train him to gait around the ring by your side at the correct pace and pattern, and to tolerate being handled and examined by the judge. Most breeds require complete dentition, all require a particular bite (scissor, level or undershot), and all males must have two apparently normal testicles fully descended into the scrotum. Enlist family and friends to hold mock trials in your garden to prepare your future champion!

Judges watch the dogs' movement very closely, believing that a properly structured animal will demonstrate soundness and conformation in his gait.

My Airedale Terrier

PUT YOUR PUPPY'S FIRST PICTURE HERE

Dog's Name _____

Date _____ Photographer _____